Direct Experience
:
Self-Realisation

अपरोक्षानुभूति

aparokṣānubhūti

said to be composed by *Ādi Śaṅkara*

translated by John M Denton with Sanskrit script, transliteration, individual word meanings and translation

Published by DFT
ISBN 978-0-9941044-9-6

Introduction

The sanskrit word for philosophy is *darśana* seeing, looking at, or the act of seeing, from the root *dṛṣ* to see. *Darśana* also means knowing, judgement, discernment, foreseeing, understanding, showing a mirror or a way of looking at the world. This book is about a different kind of seeing.
aparokṣānubhūti is the traditional name for this work and is the first word of the second verse (the first verse being the dedication).
parokṣa means other seeing or alternative perception, or indirect seeing ,
original form *paro'kṣa* from *paras* ⇒*aparaḥ* + *akṣa* (*akṣa* = eye).
Adding *a* at the beginning gives a contrary sense so
aparokṣa means direct perception, true perception or realization.
anubhūti f. perception; knowledge from any source but memory;
knowledge gained through perception by the senses (experience), inference, comparison or by verbal authority,
aparokṣānubhūti direct experience of reality i.e. self-realization.

Indirect knowledge is the cognition 'Brahman exists' as may be read in a book - the intellect is aware of the fact that Brahman is self-evident or self-revealing because it says so in a book.
Direct knowledge is such as 'I am Brahman' from experience (*anubhūti*).

Knowledge can be gained through facts such as the direct experience of 'I am Brahman' but the indirect experience remains in the realm of conjecture, supposition or theory. Hence it is a mental imagination.

The Alphabet

अ	इ	ऋ	ऌ	उ
a	*i*	*ṛ*	*ḷ*	*u*
ए	ऐ	ओ	औ	
e	*ai*	*o*	*au*	
क	च	ट	त	प
ka	*ca*	*ṭa*	*ta*	*pa*
ख	छ	ठ	थ	फ
kha	*cha*	*ṭha*	*tha*	*pha*
ग	ज	ड	द	ब
ga	*ja*	*ḍa*	*da*	*ba*
घ	झ	ढ	ध	भ
gha	*jha*	*ḍha*	*dha*	*bha*
ङ	ञ	ण	न	म
ṅa	*ña*	*ṇa*	*na*	*ma*
ह	य	र	ल	व
ha	*ya*	*ra*	*la*	*va*
	श	ष	स	
	śa	*ṣa*	*sa*	

Abbreviations

(A) to (W) references to bibliography sources

a. adjective

acc accusative case

adj adjective

adv adverb, adverbial, used adverbially

act active voice

aor aorist

At Ātmabodha

B.G. Bhagavad Gītā

comp. compound

caus causative

denom. denominative

desid desiderative

du. dual

f. feminine

ifc at the end of a compound

impf imperfect tense

impv imperative tense

ind indeclinable

inf infinitive

inv. invocation

HH His Holiness

loc locative case

m. masculine

mfn masculine, feminine or neuter = adjective

mid middle voice

n neuter gender

opt optative tense

pass passive voice

part participle

perf perfect tense

pl. plural

ppp past passive participle

pres present tense

pron pronoun

s singular

Vb. Vedabase

Ved Vedic

voc vocative case – used to address somebody (oh Rāma)

1 1st case – nominative (the subject)

2 2nd case – accusative (the object)

3 3rd case –instrumental (by or with)

4 4th case – dative (to or for something)

5 5th case- ablative (from or through)

6 6th case – genitive (of something)

7 7th case – locative (in or on something)

Pronunciation

अ a as u in but

आ ā a in master

इ i i in fix

ई ī ee in feel

उ u u in suit

ऊ ū oo in pool

ऋ ṛ ri in river

ॠ or ऋृ ṝ ri in reed

ऌ ḷ lry in jewelry

ए e a in evade

ऐ ai y in my

ओ o o in oh

औ au ou in loud

क् k k in kite

ख् kh kh in blockhead

ग् g g in good

घ् gh gh in loghouse

ङ् ṅ ng in sing

च् c ch in check

छ् ch chh in catch him

ज् j j in jam

झ jh dgeh in hedgehog

ञ् ñ n in lunch

ट् ṭ t in true

ठ् ṭh th in anthill

ड् ḍ d in drum

ढ् ḍh dh in red-haired

ण् ṇ 2nd n in none

त् t t in water

थ् th th in fat-head

द् d d in dice

ध् dh dh in adhere

न् n n in not

प् p p in put

फ् ph ph in uphill

ब् b b in bear

भ् bh bh in abhor

म् m m in mother

य् y y in you

र् r r in red

ल् l l in love

व् v w in water

श् ś sh in sure

ष् ṣ sh in show

स् s s in sit

ह् h h in hard

ं ṁ m in hum

: ḥ h in oh

श्रीहरिं परमानन्दमुपदेष्टारमीश्वरम् ।
व्यापकं सर्वलोकानां कारणं तं नमाम्यहम् ॥ १ ॥

śrīhariṁ paramānandamupadeṣṭāramīśvaram
vyāpakaṁ sarvalokānāṁ kāraṇaṁ taṁ namāmyaham

śrī hari	2/s To *śrī hari* (Kṛṣṇa, Viṣṇu, he who takes away [the heart], one who destroys (*saṁsāra*, illusion) ,
paramānandam	*2/s* supreme bliss,
upadeṣṭāra	highest teacher, first instructor,
īśvara	*Īśvara*
vyāpaka	pervading, pervader,
sarva-lokānām	of all worlds,
kāraṇa	reason, reasoning, cause,
tam	1/s/pron. to him,
namāmi	1/s/pres/act √*nam* I bow
aham	1/s/ pron. I

The following dedication begins the work –
1. "I bow to him, *śrī hari,* the supreme bliss, the highest teacher, *īśvara*, the cause and pervader of all worlds."

◘

अपरोक्षानुभूतिर्वै प्रोच्यते मोक्षसिद्धये ।

सद्भिरेव प्रयत्नेन वीक्षणीया मुहुर्मुहुः ।।२।।

aparokṣānubhūtirvai procyate mokṣasiddhaye
sadbhireva prayatnena vīkṣaṇīyā muhurmuhuḥ

aparokṣa	*1/s* direct seeing, realisation,
-anubhūtiḥ	knowledge gained by the senses, inference, comparison or verbal authority; experience, direct apprehension, experience which reveals new knowledge,
vai	*ind.* indeed,
procyate	*1/s/pres/pass. pra√uc* it is said , told forth,
mokṣa-siddhaye	for complete attainment of liberation,
sadbhiḥ	*3/pl* by the wise (pl.), by good men,
eva	indeed, only, alone,
prayatnena	3/s *prayatna* through continuous effort,
vīkṣaṇīyā	mfn is to be looked at, regarded or considered, (meditated on)
muhurmuhuḥ	again and again, repeatedly,

2. The subject of this work is the means of attaining Self-realization. It is expounded for the complete attainment of liberation. The instruction should be followed by good men (the pure in heart) with continuous effort and full attention applied again and again.

⊡

स्ववर्णाश्रमधर्मेण तपसा हरितोषणात् ।
साधनं प्रभवेत् पुंसां वैराग्यादिचतुष्टयम् ॥३॥

svavarṇāśramadharmeṇa tapasā haritoṣaṇāt
sādhanaṁ prabhavet puṁsāṁ vairāgyādicatuṣṭayam

sva-varṇa-āśrama-dharmeṇa sva own, one's own -*varṇa* class or caste, -*āśrama*-stage in the life of a Brahman

-*dharmeṇa* by duties, by carrying out the duties appropriate to one's caste, class and stage of life

tapasā by austerity

hari-toṣaṇāt *hari* the Lord, *toṣaṇa* n. the act of pleasing, satisfying, delighting, 5/s/n through propitiating the Lord,

sādhana n. means of effecting or accomplishing, an expedient, bringing about, 2/s/n the means of attaining,

prabhavet 1/s/opt *pra*√*bhū* he/it should arise, originate from, be able to, appear,

puṁsām 6/pl/m of men

vairāgya-ādi *vairāgya* 'the power of detachment', indifference, *ādi* beginning with,

catuṣṭayam *catuṣṭaya* fourfold

3. The means through which men may attain the four-fold initial qualifications, (are explained) starting with *vairāgya* (detachment). (The aspirant) should continue to carry out his duties, practice austerity and please the Lord.

this refers to the traditional 4 preliminary qualifications for higher knowledge the first of which is *vairāgya* and the others are *viveka* discrimination, *mumukṣutva* earnest desire for liberation and *śama* -the six treasures [*śama* the tranquillity brought about by loss of inherent desires, *dama* control of the senses, *uparati* self-withdrawal - desisting from unnecessary activity, ultimately "the mind-function ceasing to act by means of external objects", *titikṣa* forbearance, endurance, patience, *śraddhā* faith established through reason and experience, *samādhāna* mental balance through perfected concentration, 'But by perceiving objects with organs that are free from attraction and repulsion and are under his own control, the self-controlled man attains serenity). B.G. 2.64 Gam.],

⊡

ब्रह्मादिस्थावरान्तेषु वैराग्यं विषयेष्वनु ।

यथैव काकविष्ठायां वैराग्यं तद्धि निर्मलम् ।।४।।

brahmādisthāvarānteṣu vairāgyaṁ viṣayeṣvanu

yathaiva kākaviṣṭhāyāṁ vairāgyaṁ taddhi nirmalam

brahma- from Brahma,

-ādi in the beginning,

-sthāvara to inanimate objects

-anteṣu in the end (pl.),

vairāgya detachment, the power of detachment,

viṣayeṣu 7/pl/m in objects, objects of sense, anything perceptible,

a*nu* ind. according to, in regard to,

yathaiva just as,

kāka crow, *-viṣṭhāyāṁ* excrement 6/pl,

vairāgyam *2/s* detachment,

tat *pron.* that,

hi *ind.* for, because, on account of, just, pray, do, indeed

nirmala *mfn* spotless, bright, pure, clean, shining,

4. Just as one is indifferent to something (as insignificant as) crow-droppings so such detachment (applied) to everything from the world of Brahmā in the beginning to inanimate objects in the end is pure *vairāgya.*

Detachment needs to be complete to be effective. As bird excrement may be perceived but cause no movement in the mind so the mind of the aspirant needs to settle. *Vairāgya* mentioned in the previous verse has now been described with regard to purity and fulness. This must be explored, discussed, honed, practiced diligently and perfected. The other qualities in verse 3 are now described.

回

नित्यमात्मस्वरूपं हि दृश्यं तद्विपरीतगम् ।
एवं यो निश्चयः सम्यग्विवेको वस्तुनः स वै ॥५॥

nityamātmasvarūpaṁ hi dṛśyaṁ tadviparītagam
evaṁ yo niścayaḥ samyagviveko vastunaḥ sa vai

nitya	eternal,
-ātma-svarūpa	own form, self, own nature
hi	or, because, on account of, indeed,
dṛśya	the seen, the visible, to be looked at, worth seeing,
tat	that
viparītaga	gone backwards or in a reverse direction, contrary
evam	thus,
yaḥ	who, which,
niścaya	inquiry, fixed opinion, certainty, conviction, aim,
samyak	going along with or together, combined, united, accurate, proper, true,
vivekaḥ	discrimination, distinction,
vastunaḥ -	*vastu* the real, that which truly exists, i.e. is permanent 5/6/s/n
sa	that *vai* indeed,

5. The Atman in itself is certainly eternal, the visible is that which is the contrary. Who knows this with certainty properly discriminates that which truly exists (and this is called viveka).

सदैव वासनात्यागः शमोऽयमिति शब्दितः ।
निग्रहो बाह्यवृत्तीनां दम इत्यभिधीयते ॥६॥

sadaiva vāsanātyāgaḥ śamo'yamiti śabditaḥ
nigraho bāhyavṛttīnāṁ dama ityabhidhīyate

sadaiva	always, at all times,
vāsanā-	the impression of anything remaining unconsciously in the mind, present consciousness of past perceptions, latent tendencies,
tyāgaḥ	leaving, abandoning, forsaking,
śamaḥ	tranquillity, calmness, rest,
ayam	this, *iti* end of quote, thus, in this manner,
śabditaḥ	sounded, cried, uttered, imparted, communicated,
nigrahaḥ	suppression, restraint,
bāhya	external, outer, exterior,
vṛttīnām	6/pl. of general usage, common practice, mode of being, nature, state, activity, function, mood (of the mind),
dama	self control, the control of the organs of action,
iti	see above,
abhidhīyate	it is called or explained,

6. The abandonment at all times of latent tendencies and impressions that remain unconsciously in the mind is called *śama* which means tranquillity, calmness and rest. The restraint of the external organs of action is called *dama* or self-control.

विषयेभ्यः परावृत्तिः परमोपरतिर्हि सा ।
सहनं सर्वदुःखानां तितिक्षा सा शुभा मता ।।७।।

viṣayebhyaḥ parāvṛttiḥ paramoparatirhi sā
sahanaṁ sarvaduḥkhānāṁ titikṣā sā śubhā matā

viṣayebhyaḥ	for or from sense-objects
parāvṛttiḥ	f. turning back or round, returning,
paramā	highest, most prominent,
-uparatiḥ	f. cessation, stopping, desisting from sensual enjoyment (spontaneously),
hi	for, because, on account of,
sā	she, that,
sahana	patient, patient endurance,
sarvaduḥkhānāṁ	of all sorrow or misery,
titikṣā	forbearance, endurance, patience,
sā	she, that,
śubhā	pure, unmixed, auspicious, fortunate,
matā	mfn thought, believed, imagined, understood, regarded or considered as, taken as or passing for,

7. The highest form of turning aside from sense-objects is called *uparati* (natural disengagement from sensual enjoyment). Patient endurance of all sorrow or misery is regarded as *titikṣā* (forbearance, endurance, patience).

निगमाचार्यवाक्येषु भक्तिः श्रद्धेति विश्रुता ।
चित्तैकाग्र्यं तु सल्लक्ष्ये समाधानमिति स्मृतम् ॥८॥

nigamācāryavākyeṣu bhaktiḥ śraddheti viśrutā
cittaikāgryaṁ tu sallakṣye samādhānamiti smṛtam

nigama	the Veda or Vedic text 6/pl,
-ācārya	spiritual guide or teacher 6/pl
-vākyeṣu	in the words 7/pl (in the words of the Vedas and teachers),
bhaktiḥ	faith or love or devotion,
śraddha (ā)	faith
iti	end of quote,
viśrutā	known as, named,
citta	mind, memory, attending 6/s
ekāgrya (or aikāgrya)	close attention, concentration on one object, (concentration of the mind)
-tu	but, and,
-sallakṣye (sat-lakṣye)	good aim, right aim or object 7/s (*sat* representing existence as Brahman),
samādhānam	profound absorption or contemplation,
iti	thus, end of quote,
smṛtam	recognized, remembered, known (as),

8. Faith in the words of the Vedas and of the spiritual teachers who teach them is called *śraddhā.* And single-pointed concentration of the mind on the right object (as Brahman) is known as *samādhāna.*

संसारबंधनिर्मुक्तिः कथं मे स्यात् कदा विधे ।
इति या सुदृढा बुदधिर्वक्तव्या सा मुमुक्षुता ।।९।।

saṁsārabaṁdhanirmuktiḥ kathaṁ me syāt kadā vidhe
iti yā sudṛḍhā buddhirvaktavyā sā mumukṣutā

saṁsāra	-undergoing transmigration, worldly illusion, *baṁdha-(bandha)*- a bond, tie, fetter,
nirmukti	f. deliverance from, liberation, freedom from the bonds of transmigration,
kathaṁ	how,
me	my
syāt	perchance, it may be, perhaps,
kadā	when
vidhe	O Creator,
iti	end of quotation,
yā	that which, such
sudṛḍhā	well secured, very firm or hard or strong,
buddhiḥ	intelligence,
vaktavyā	to be spoken, said or declared, to be named or called,
sā	she, that
mumukṣutā	desire for liberation or final emancipation

9. 'How and when may there be freedom from the bonds of worldly illusion, O Creator?' When such a desire is very strong in the *buddhi* this is called *mumukṣutā* (desire for liberation).

उक्तसाधनयुक्तेन विचारः पुरुषेण हि ।

कर्तव्यो ज्ञानसिद्ध्यर्थमात्मनः शुभमिच्छता ॥१०॥

uktasādhanayuktena vicāraḥ puruṣeṇa hi

kartavyo jñānasiddhyarthamātmanaḥ śubhamicchatā

ukta - uttered, said, spoken,

sādhana - the act of mastering, accomplishment, *yuktena* properly, suitably (qualified)

vicāraḥ puruṣeṇa Self-inquiry (inquiry with the Self),

hi for|

kartavyaḥ to be done

jñānasiddhyarthamātmanaḥ

jñāna- n. higher knowledge, awareness,

-siddhi -artham- 2/s mfn whose goal has been achieved, he who has fulfilled the object,

-ātmanaḥ 6/s/m of the Self

leading to the goal of knowledge of the Self

śubham icchatā pure desire

10. Only he who has mastered the qualifications for knowledge spoken of in the previous verses is considered suitably qualified to study with pure desire the subject of Self-inquiry leading to the goal of knowledge of the Self.

◻

नोत्पद्यते विना ज्ञानं विचारेणान्यसाधनैः ।
यथा पदार्थभानं हि प्रकाशेन विना क्वचित् ।।११।।

notpadyate vinā jñānaṁ vicāreṇānyasādhanaiḥ
yathā padārthabhānaṁ hi prakāśena vinā kvacit

na	not
utpadyate	is produced or originated,
vinā	without, except, exclusive of
jñānam	higher knowledge
vicāreṇa	by, with, through inquiry,
anya-sādhanaiḥ	by, through other means,
yathā	as , like, according as, so that,
padārtha	- the meaning of a word, that which corresponds to the meaning of a word, a thing, material object, a principle,
bhāna	appearance, evidence, perception, light, lustre, (perception of things, the meanings of words, of the relationships of things and words),
hi	for, because, on account of,
prakāśena	by, with, through, visible, shining, bright, light, elucidation, explanation,
vinā	without,
kvacit	somewhere, at any time, in any circumstances,

11. Higher knowledge is not produced by any other means but enquiry just as objects are not perceived without light.

कोऽहं कथमिदं जातं को वै कर्ताऽस्य विद्यते ।
उपादानं किमस्तीह विचारः सोऽयमीदृशः ॥१२॥

ko'haṁ kathamidaṁ jātaṁ ko vai kartā'sya vidyate
upādānaṁ kimastīha vicāraḥ so'yamīdṛśaḥ

kaḥ	who,
aham	I
katham	how,
idam	this,
jātam	brought into existence, produced, caused, appeared,
kaḥ	who,
vai	indeed
kartā	the creator,
asya	of this
vidyate	is known, is discovered,
upādānam	material of any kind,
kim	what *asti* is
iha	here, in this world,
vicāraḥ	inquiry,
saḥ	he , that,
ayam	this
īdṛśaḥ	endowed with such qualities, nature, such,

12. Who am I? How is this brought into existence? Who is the Creator of this? What is it's material cause? That is the nature of this enquiry.

नाहं भूतगणो देहो नाहं चाक्षगणस्तथा ।

एतद्विलक्षणः कश्चिद्विचारः सोऽयमीदृशः ॥१३॥

nāhaṁ bhūtagaṇo deho nāhaṁ cākṣagaṇastathā
etadvilakṣaṇaḥ kaścidvicāraḥ so'yamīdṛśaḥ

na ahaṁ	not I,
bhūtagaṇaḥ	the host of living beings, a multitude of spirits or ghosts, a combination of the elements,
dehaḥ	the body,
nāham	not I, *ca* and, so,
akṣa-gaṇaḥ	(*akṣa* - the eye but often used to represent all senses, *gaṇa* - an assemblage) , an assemblage of the senses,
tathā	so, such, thus, also,
etad	- 5/pl. from these,
-vilakṣaṇaḥ	different, having different marks, varying in character, state or condition without distinctive mark, the act of distinguishing,
kaścid	someone, something, somebody,
vicāraḥ	inquiry,
saḥ	he, that, *ayam* this (indefinite)
īdṛśaḥ	such, of this sort, of this kind,

13. I am not a combination of the elements. I am not the body nor a collection of senses. Thus I am something different from these. This is the method of inquiry about That.

अज्ञानप्रभवं सर्वं ज्ञानेन प्रविलीयते ।
संकल्पो विविधः कर्ता विचारः सोऽयमीदृशः ।।१४।।

ajñānaprabhavaṁ sarvaṁ jñānena pravilīyate
saṁkalpo vividhaḥ kartā vicāraḥ so'yamīdṛśaḥ

ajñāna	ignorance,
prabhavam	prominent, origin, cause of existence,
sarvam	all,
jñānena	by or through knowledge,
pravilīyate	is dissolved,
saṁkalpaḥ	resolution, idea, notion, will, desire,
vividhaḥ	of various sorts, manifold,
kartā	the doer, creator,
vicāraḥ	inquiry
saḥ	he, that,
ayam	this
dṛśaḥ	such, of this sort, of this kind,

14. Ignorance causes things to exist.
(but) through knowledge it is dissolved.
Mental activity of many kinds is the source of ignorance.
This is the way of inquiry about That.

एतयोर्यदुपादानमेकं सूक्ष्मं सदव्ययम् ।
यथैव मृद्घटादीनां विचारः सोऽयमीदृशः ॥१५॥

etayoryadupādānamekaṁ sūkṣmaṁ sadavyayam
yathaiva mṛdghaṭādīnāṁ vicāraḥ so'yamīdṛśaḥ

etayoḥ	of these two,
yat	who, which,
upādānam	material of any kind, material cause,
ekam	one, alone, only,
sūkṣmam	subtle, intangible,
sat	existence
avyayam	imperishable,
yathaiva	just as
mṛt	earth
ghaṭa- ādīnāṁ	(pot -beginning with 6/pl) from pots and the like,
vicāraḥ	enquiry,
saḥ	he, that,
ayam	this
īdṛśaḥ	of this sort or kind,

15. The material cause of these two (ignorance and mental activity) is that one, subtle, existence; just as earth is the material cause of pots and the like. This is the nature of the inquiry.

Note The material cause: "that out of which", e.g., the bronze of a statue.

अहमेकोऽपि सूक्ष्मश्च ज्ञाता साक्षी सदव्ययः ।

तदहं नात्र सन्देहो विचारः सोऽयमीदृशः ।।१६।।

ahameko'pi sūkṣmaśca jñātā sākṣī sadavyayaḥ
tadahaṁ nātra sandeho vicāraḥ so'yamīdṛśaḥ

aham	I,
ekaḥ	one,
api	also,
sūkṣmaḥ	subtle,
ca	and
jñātā	known, comprehended, perceived, understood, f. intelligence,
sākṣī	the witness
sat	existence,
avyayaḥ	undecaying,
tat	that,
aham	I,
na	not,
atra	here,
sandehaḥ	doubt, ambiguity, uncertainty,
vicāraḥ	enquiry,
saḥ	he, that,
ayam	this
īdṛśaḥ	of this sort or kind, such,

16. I am the One, the Subtle, the Conscious Intelligence, the Witness, and the Undecaying Existence. I am, without doubt, That. Such is the nature of this enquiry.

आतमा विनिष्कलो ह्येको देहो बहुभिरावृतः ।
तयोरैक्यं प्रपश्यन्ति किमज्ञानमतः परम् ।।१७।।

ātmā viniṣkalo hyeko deho bahubhirāvṛtaḥ
tayoraikyaṁ prapaśyanti kimajñānamataḥ param

ātmā	the Self
viniṣkalaḥ	undivided, without parts,
hi	for, because, on account of,
ekaḥ	one, only, alone,
dehaḥ	the body
bahubhiḥ	with many 3/pl,
āvṛtaḥ	abounding with, filled with,
tayoḥ	of/in these two
aikyam	oneness, unity, sameness, harmony, identity,
prapaśyanti	they see before their eyes, behold,
kim	who? what?
ajñānam	ignorance,
ataḥ	therefore, hence, now, so,
param	other,
ataḥ param	hereafter, thereafter, henceforth,

17. The Self is undivided, one alone, without parts while the body has many. People see only oneness in these two. Is it any wonder that consequently the result is ignorance?

आत्मा नियामकश्चान्तर्देहो बाह्यो नियम्यकः ।
तयोरैक्यं प्रपश्यन्ति किमज्ञानमतः परम् ॥१८॥

ātmā niyāmakaścāntardeho bāhyo niyamyakaḥ
tayoraikyaṁ prapaśyanti kimajñānamataḥ param

ātmā	the Self
niyāmakaḥ	a guide or ruler
ca	and,
antaḥ	inner,
dehaḥ	body,
bāhyaḥ	outer,
niyamyakaḥ	the ruled,
tayoḥ	of/in these two
aikyam	oneness, unity, sameness, harmony, identity,
prapaśyanti	they see before their eyes, behold,
kim	who? what? wherefore? whence? why?
ajñānam	ignorance,
ataḥ	therefore, hence, now, so,
param	other,
ataḥ param	hereafter, thereafter, henceforth,

18. The Self is the inner ruler. The body is the outer and the ruled. People see only oneness in these two. Is it any wonder that the result is ignorance?

आत्मा ज्ञानमयः पुण्यो देहो मांसमयोऽशुचिः ।
तयोरैक्यं प्रपश्यन्ति किमज्ञानमतः परम् ॥१९॥

ātmā jñānamayaḥ puṇyo deho māṁsamayo'śuciḥ
tayoraikyaṁ prapaśyanti kimajñānamataḥ param

ātmā	the Self
jñānamayaḥ	consisting of knowledge,
puṇyaḥ	holy, pure, meritorious, auspicious, good, sacred,
dehaḥ	the body,
māṁsamayaḥ	consisting of flesh,
aśuci	impure, foul,
tayoḥ	of/in these two
aikyam	oneness, unity, sameness, harmony, identity,
prapaśyanti	they see before their eyes, behold,
kim	who? what? wherefore? whence? why?
ajñānam	ignorance,
ataḥ	therefore, hence, now, so,
param	other,
	ataḥ param (is a phrase) hereafter, thereafter, henceforth,

19. The Self is sacred pure knowledge. The body is made of flesh and impure. People see only oneness in these two. Is it any wonder that the result is ignorance?

आत्मा प्रकाशकः स्वच्छो देहस्तामस उच्यते ।
तयोरैक्यं प्रपश्यन्ति किमज्ञानमतः परम् ॥२०॥

ātmā prakāśakaḥ svaccho dehastāmasa ucyate
tayoraikyaṁ prapaśyanti kimajñānamataḥ param

ātmā	the Self
prakāśakaḥ	the discoverer, the sun, the illuminator, universally known, brilliant, illustrating,
svacchaḥ	clean, transparent, very clear,
dehaḥ	the body
tāmasa	having the nature of darkness, dark, ignorant, sleep,
ucyate	it is said,
tayoḥ	of/in these two
aikyam	oneness, unity, sameness, harmony, identity,
prapaśyanti	they see before their eyes, behold,
kim	who? what? wherefore? whence? why?
ajñānam	ignorance,
ataḥ param	hereafter, thereafter, henceforth,

20. The Self is the illuminator, brilliant, transparent and clear. The body is said to have the nature of darkness, ignorance and sleep. People see only oneness in these two. Is it any wonder that the result is ignorance?

आत्मा नित्यो हि सद्रूपो देहोऽनित्यो ह्यसन्मय : ।
तयोरैक्यं प्रपश्यन्ति किमज्ञानमतः परम् ।।२१।।

ātmā nityo hi sadrūpo deho'nityo hyasanmayaḥ
tayoraikyaṁ prapaśyanti kimajñānamataḥ param

ātmā	the Self,
nityaḥ	eternal,
hi	for, because, on account of,
sadrūpo	reality,
dehaḥ anityaḥ	the body not eternal, transient,
hi	for, since etc.
asat-mayaḥ	non-existent, unreal
tayoḥ	of/in these two
aikyam	oneness, unity, sameness, harmony, identity,
prapaśyanti	they see before their eyes, behold,
kim	who? what?
ajñānam	ignorance,
ataḥ param	hereafter, thereafter, henceforth,

21. The Self has reality because it is eternal. The body is called unreal because it is transient. People see only oneness in these two. Is it any wonder that the result is ignorance?

आतमानस्तत्प्रकाशत्वं यत्पदार्थावभासनम् ।
नगन्यादिदीप्तिवद्दीप्तिर्भवत्यान्ध्यं यतो निशि ।।२२।।

ātmānastatprakāśatvaṁ yatpadārthāvabhāsanam
nāgnyādidīptivaddīptirbhavatyāndhyaṁ yato niśi

ātmānaḥ	of the Self *tat* that
prakāśatvam	clearness, brightness, appearance, manifestation, renown,
yat	who, which, what,
pada-artha-avabhāsanam	
	padārtha that which corresponds to the meaning of a word, a thing, material object,
avabhāsanam	shining, becoming manifest, illuminating,
na	not,
agni -ādi-dīptivat	*agni* - fire,
	ādi- beginning with
	dīptivat like brightness, light, splendour, beauty,
	dīptiḥ brightness, light, splendour, beauty,
bhavati	he/it becomes,
āndhyam	blindness, darkness,
yataḥ	because, since, for
niśi	at night,

22. The illumination of the Self is that which corresponds to the manifestation of (all) material things. That splendour is not like the brightness of fire and the like for these are subject to (change with) the darkness of night.

देहोऽहमित्ययं मूढो धृत्वा तिष्ठत्यहो जनः ।
ममायमित्यपि ज्ञात्वा घटद्रष्टेव सर्वदा ।।२३।।

deho'hamityayaṁ mūḍho dhṛtvā tiṣṭhatyaho janaḥ
mamāyamityapi jñātvā ghaṭadrṣṭeva sarvadā

dehaḥ	the body,
aham	I (am)
iti	end of quote,
ayam	this
mūḍhaḥ	ignorant,
dhṛtvā	having held or borne, held fast, assuming this form,
tiṣṭhati	he stands, remains, stays, continues,
aho	oh, alas,
janaḥ	man
mama	my, mine, of me,
ayam	this,
iti	end of quote, thus,
api	also, even,
jñātvā	having known or understood, knowing,
ghaṭa-drṣṭeva	*(ghaṭa-drṣṭa-iva* pot-seen-as if, like,*)* as if a person seeing a pot,
sarvadā	at all times, ever, forever,

23. Alas, that a man continues to hold the ignorant view "I am this body", while he is aware that it is just something he is attached to just as someone seeing a pot understands it is just a pot.

ब्रह्मैवाहं समः शान्तः सच्चिदानन्दलक्षणः।
नाहं देहो ह्यसद्रूपो ज्ञानमित्युच्यते बुधैः ।।२४।।

brahmaivāhaṁ samaḥ śāntaḥ saccidānandalakṣaṇaḥ
nāhaṁ deho hyasadrūpo jñānamityucyate budhaiḥ

brahma	in comp. for Brahman, the one self-existent Spirit, the Absolute,
-eva	ind. indeed,
-aham	pron. 1/s, I (am)
samaḥ	adj. 1/s, equanimous, same, equal in all respects,
śāntaḥ	adj. 1/s peaceful, calm, undisturbed,
sat	*pres. part.* existence, good, living, present, wise,
cid	*adj.* consciousness, pure uninfluenced consciousness,
ānanda	1/s/m bliss,
lakṣaṇaḥ	mfn indicating, expressing indirectly, characteristic, attribute,
na aham	not I
dehaḥ	the body 1/s/m
hi	ind. for because, since,
asat	pres.part. non-existent,
rūpaḥ	1/s/ suffix, form, shape, figure, (as suffix) consisting of,
jñānam	2/s/n knowledge, higher knowledge,
iti	end of quote,
ucyate	it is said, 1/s/pres/act/√*vac*
budhaiḥ	3/s/ adj. m. by the wise,

24. I am indeed the Brahman - the same in all respects, undisturbed, associated with the characteristics of existence, consciousness and bliss. I am not the body for form is illusory. The wise say this is true knowledge.

निर्विकारो निराकारो निरवद्योऽहमव्ययः ।
नाहं देहो ह्यसद्रूपो ज्ञानमित्युच्यते बुधैः ।।२५।।

nirvikāro nirākāro niravadyo'hamavyayaḥ
nāhaṁ deho hyasadrūpo jñānamityucyate budhaiḥ

nirvikāraḥ	unchanged, unchangeable, uniform, normal,
nirākāraḥ	formless, shapeless, incorporeal (brahman), making no appearance or show,
niravadyaḥ	unblamable, unobjectionable, blamelessness, excellence,
aham	I
avyayaḥ	imperishable, undecaying,
na aham	not I
dehaḥ	the body
hi	for because, since,
asat	non-existent,
rūpaḥ	form, shape, figure,
jñānam	knowledge,
iti	end of quote,
ucyate	it is said,
budhaiḥ	by the wise,

25. I am imperishable, unchangeable, incorporeal and without blemish. I am not the body for form is illusory. The wise say this is true knowledge.

निरामयो निराभासो निर्विकल्पोऽहमाततः ।
नाहं देहो ह्यसद्रूपो ज्ञानमित्युच्यते बुधैः ॥२६॥

nirāmayo nirābhāso nirvikalpo'hamātataḥ
nāhaṁ deho hyasadrūpo jñānamityucyate budhaiḥ

nirāmayaḥ	without disease,
nirābhāsaḥ	without fallacious appearance, imageless, beyond comprehension,
nirvikalpaḥ	free from change or differences, not admitting an alternative, admitting no doubt, not wavering,
aham	I
ātataḥ	spread, extended, all-pervading,
na aham	not I
dehaḥ	the body
hi	for because, since,
asat	non-existent,
rūpaḥ	form, shape, figure,
jñānam	knowledge,
iti	end of quote,
ucyate	it is said,
budhaiḥ	by the wise,

26. I am free from disease, beyond comprehension, unchangeable and all-pervading. I am not the body for form is illusory. It is said by the wise that this is true knowledge.

निर्गुणो निष्क्रियो नित्यो नित्यमुक्तोऽहमच्युतः ।

नाहं देहो ह्यसद्रूपो ज्ञानमित्युच्यते बुधैः ॥२७॥

nirguṇo niṣkriyo nityo nityamukto'hamacyutaḥ

nāhaṁ deho hyasadrūpo jñānamityucyate budhaiḥ

nirguṇaḥ	devoid of all qualities or properties,
niṣkriyaḥ	actionless
nityaḥ	eternal,
nityamuktaḥ	ever free,
aham	I
acyutaḥ	imperishable,
na aham	not I
dehaḥ	the body
hi	for because, since,
asat	non-existent,
rūpaḥ	form, shape, figure,
jñāmam	knowledge,
iti	end of quote,
ucyate	it is said,
budhaiḥ	by the wise,

27. I am without attributes, actionless, eternal, ever-free and imperishable. I am not the body for form is illusory. It is said by the wise that this is true knowledge.

निर्मलो निश्चलोऽनन्तः शुद्धोऽहमजरोऽमरः ।
नाहं देहो ह्यसद्रूपो ज्ञानमित्युच्यते बुधैः ॥२८॥

nirmalo niścalo'nantaḥ śuddho'hamajaro'maraḥ
nāhaṁ deho hyasadrūpo jñānamityucyate budhaiḥ

nirmalaḥ	spotless, clean, pure, shining, sinless, virtuous,
niścalaḥ	motionless, immovable, invariable, unchangeable,
anantaḥ	endless, boundless, eternal, infinite,
śuddhaḥ	clean, pure, clear, faultless,
aham	I,
ajaraḥ	undecaying, ever young,
amaraḥ	undying, immortal, imperishable,
na aham	not I
dehaḥ	the body
hi	for because, since,
asat	non-existent,
rūpaḥ	form, shape, figure,
jñāmam	knowledge,
iti	end of quote,
ucyate	it is said,
budhaiḥ	by the wise,

28. I am immortal, undecaying, taintless, immovable, infinite and pure. I am not the body for form is illusory. It is said by the wise that this is true knowledge.

स्वदेहे शोभनं सन्तं पुरुषाख्यं च संमतम् ।
किं मूर्ख शून्यमात्मानं देहातीतं करोषि भोः ॥२९॥

svadehe śobhanaṁ santaṁ puruṣākhyaṁ ca saṁmatam
kiṁ mūrkha śūnyamātmānaṁ dehātītaṁ karoṣi bhoḥ

svadehe	in own body
śobhanam	brilliant, splendid, beautiful, propitious, auspicious,
santam	existent, (2/s/m, *sat)*
puruṣa -ākhyam	named, called or known as the Self,
ca	and
saṁmatam	agreed, highly honoured, approved, considered or regarded as, accepted as,
kiṁ	what? why?
mūrkha	stupid, dull, foolish, voc. O foolish one,
śūnyam	zero, void, vacant, empty,
ātmānam	the Self,
deha	the body,
atītam	passed away, past, negligent, dead, one who has gone through or got over or beyond,
karoṣi	you make, do,
bhoḥ	O!, Ho!

29. In your own body is that which is splendid, existent, known and established as the Self. Why, O foolish one, do you act as if the transcendent Self is missing from the inert body.

⧈

स्वात्मानं शृणु मूर्ख त्वं श्रुत्या युक्त्या च पुरुषम् ।
देहातीतं सदाकारं सुदुर्दर्शं भवादृशैः ॥३०॥

svātmānaṁ śṛṇu mūrkha tvaṁ śrutyā yuktyā ca puruṣam
dehātītaṁ sadākāraṁ sudurdarśaṁ bhavādṛśaiḥ

sva-ātmānaṁ	own self
śṛṇu	listen, hear, realize,
mūrkha	O fool, blockhead,
tvam	you
śrutyā	by or through
śruti	words of revealed verbal revelation, verbal testimony,
yuktyā	by or through reason,
ca	and,
puruṣam	the Self,
deha	the body
-ātītam	passed away, past, negligent, dead, one who has gone through or got over or beyond,
sat	being, existing, occurring, happening, being present, abiding in
-ākāram	form, shape, figure, appearance, (present in the form)
sudurdarśam	very difficult to be discerned, seen or observed,
bhavādṛśaiḥ	by any (3/pl.) like you 749/3

30. Realize your own self O fool. Through revealed knowledge and through reason (know) that transcendent Self abiding in the form of the otherwise dead body. It is very difficult to discern by any like you.

◙

अहंशब्देन विख्यात एक एव स्थितः परः ।

स्थूलस्त्वनेकतां प्राप्तः कथं स्याद्देहकः पुमान् ॥३१॥

ahaṁśabdena vikhyāta eka eva sthitaḥ paraḥ

sthūlastvanekatāṁ prāptaḥ kathaṁ syāddehakaḥ pumān

aham	I,
śabdena	by words or speech,
vikhyāta	known as, called, named, famous, celebrated,
eka	one, only, alone,
eva	indeed,
sthitaḥ	standing, existing, abiding in,
paraḥ	other, beyond,
sthūlaḥ	large, thick, stout, dull, stupid, ignorant,
tu	but,
anekatām	muchness, manifold condition,
prāptaḥ	arrived at, reached, acquired,
katham	how,
syāt	it may be, it could be, perchance, 1/s/opt/act,
dehakaḥ	the body,
pumān	men, man? the Absolute person,

31. Known in speech as 'I', one alone indeed, existing beyond ignorance. ow could it be this manifest diversity (of bodies) ? How could the body be the *Puruṣa*, I ?

⊡

अहं द्रष्टृतया सिद्धो देहो दृश्यतया स्थितः ।
ममायमिति निर्देशात् कथं स्याद्देहकः पुमान् ।।३२।।

ahaṁ draṣṭṛtayā siddho deho dṛśyatayā sthitaḥ
mamāyamiti nirdeśāt kathaṁ syāddehakaḥ pumān

aham	I,
draṣṭṛ	-the seer, beholder, one who sees,
-tayā	by or with that or her, through which, by whom,
siddhaḥ	successful, accomplished, fulfilled, established, settled, proven,
dehaḥ	the body,
dṛśya	any visible object, the visible world,
-tayā	by or with that or her,
sthitaḥ	standing, situated, resting or abiding in,
mama	my
ayam	this, (this is my or mine),
iti	end of quote,
nirdeśāt	5/s from this description,
kathaṁ	how?
syāt	it could be, it should be, (opt), √*as*
dehakaḥ	the body,
pumān	Puruṣa

32. ‘*Aham*’ is the seer by whom (perception) is fulfilled. The body is an object through which it is present. This is indicated when we say about the body “This is mine”. How then could the body be the *Puruṣa*?

अहं विकारहीनस्तु देहो नित्यं विकारवान् ।
इति प्रतीयते साक्षात् कथं स्याद्देहकः पुमान् ॥३३॥

ahaṁ vikārahīnastu deho nityaṁ vikāravān
iti pratīyate sākṣāt kathaṁ syāddehakaḥ pumān

aham	I,
vikāra	change of form or nature, transformation,
hīnaḥ	left, abandoned, forsaken, left out, wanting, omitted,
tu	but,
dehaḥ	the body,
nityam	eternal, forever,
vikāravān	having change of form or nature,
iti	end of quote,
pratīyate	is recognized,
sākṣāt	visibly, direct, in the presence of, apparently, in sight of, in person,
katham	how,
syāt	it could be, it should be,
dehakaḥ	the body,
pumān	the Puruṣa

33. I (*Aham*) is without change of form or nature but the body is ever changing. How could that which is visibly recognized as the body be the *Puruṣa*?

⊡

यस्मात् परमिति श्रुत्या तया पुरुषलक्षणम् ।
विनिर्णीतं विमूढेन कथं स्याद्देहकः पुमान् ।।३४।।

yasmāt paramiti śrutyā tayā puruṣalakṣaṇam
vinirṇītaṁ vimūḍhena kathaṁ syāddehakaḥ pumān

yasmāt	from which, than which,
param	farther than, beyond, "there is nothing higher"
iti	end of quote,
śrutyā	by *śruti (*text),
tayā	by that,
puruṣa-lakṣaṇam	indicating, expressing indirectly, characteristic, attribute, nature, (the nature of the *Puruṣa,)* 2/s
vinirṇītam	determined clearly, ascertained, 2/s,
vimūḍhena	(by the) not foolish, a kind of divine being, 3/s,
katham	how,
syāt	it could be, it should be,
dehakaḥ	the body,
pumān	the Puruṣa

34. It is determined clearly by the wise and shown by the *śruti* text that - "There is nothing higher" than the nature of the *Puruṣa.* So how could the body be the *Puruṣa?*

⊡

सर्वं पुरुष एवेति सूक्ते पुरुषसंज्ञिते ।
अप्युच्यते यतः श्रुत्या कथं स्याद्देहकः पुमान् ।।३५।।

sarvaṁ puruṣa eveti sūkte puruṣasaṁjñite
apyucyate yataḥ śrutyā kathaṁ syāddehakaḥ pumān

sarvam	all,
puruṣa	Puruṣa,
eva	indeed,
iti	end of quote,
sūkte	well or properly said or recited, wise saying,
puruṣa	Puruṣa
saṁjñite	7/s in the communicated, named
api	also, moreover,
ucyate	is said, is called,
yataḥ	from, from whom, because,
śrutyā	by the *śruti*,
katham	how,
syāt	it could be, it should be,
dehakaḥ	the body,
pumān	the Puruṣa

35. "All this is indeed the *Puruṣa.*" This is stated in the well-known hymn from the ṛgveda called the *Puruṣa Sukta*. Since this has the authority of śruti how then could the body be the *Puruṣa*?

असङ्गः पुरुषः प्रोक्तो बृहदारण्यकेऽपि च ।
अनन्तमलसंश्लिष्टः कथं स्याद्देहकः पुमान् ।।

asaṅgaḥ puruṣaḥ prokto bṛhadāraṇyake'pi ca
anantamalasaṁśliṣṭaḥ kathaṁ syāddehakaḥ pumān

asaṅgaḥ	unattached,
puruṣaḥ	Puruṣa,
proktaḥ	taught, said, told,
bṛhadāraṇyake	in the Bṛhadāraṇyaka Upaniṣad,
api	also
ca	and
ananta	endless,
-mala	filth, dust, impurity
-saṁśliṣṭaḥ	closely blended together,
-katham	how
syāt	it could be, it should be,
-dehakaḥ	the body,
-pumān	the Puruṣa

36. It is also declared in the *Bṛhadāraṇyaka Upaniṣad* that the Self is unattached. So how could this body which is a mass of impurities be considered to be the *Puruṣa?*

तत्रैव च समाख्यातः स्वयंज्योतिर्हि पुरुषः।

जडः परप्रकाश्योऽयं कथं स्याद्देहकः पुमान् ।।३७।।

tatraiva ca samākhyātaḥ svayaṁjyotirhi puruṣaḥ

jaḍaḥ paraprakāśyo'yaṁ kathaṁ syāddehakaḥ pumān

tatra	there, in that place,
eva	indeed, very
ca	and, also, again, moreover,
samākhyātaḥ	explained, declared, related
svayam	own self-
-jyotiḥ	light, illumination
-hi	on account of, for, because, since,
puruṣaḥ	puruṣa, the Self,
jaḍaḥ	cold, frigid, apathetic, inanimate, unintelligent, inert,
para	other
-prakāśyaḥ	to be brought to light or made manifest (illuminated or made manifest by other means),
-ayam	this,
-katham	how
-syāt	it could be, it should be,
-dehakaḥ	the body,
-pumān	the Puruṣa

37. Moreover in the same place it says that the Self is self-illuminating. How could the body be the *Puruṣa* since it is insentient and must be illuminated by other than itself?

प्रोक्तोऽपि कर्मकाण्डेन ह्यात्मा देहाद्विलक्षणः ।
नित्यश्च तत्फलं भुंक्ते देहपातादनन्तरम् ॥३८॥

prokto'pi karmakāṇḍena hyātmā dehādvilakṣaṇaḥ
nityaśca tatphalaṁ bhuṁkte dehapātādanantaram

proktaḥ	told, taught, said, spoken,
api	also, moreover,
karmakāṇḍena	by the Karmakāṇḍa *(*a part of the Veda relating to ceremonial acts and sacrificial rites*),*
hi	for, since, because, on account of,
ātmā	the Self,
dehāt	from the body,
vilakṣaṇaḥ	different, differing from, various, perceiving, seeing,
nityaḥ	eternal, ever, permanent,
ca	and
tatphalam	fruit of that
bhuṁkte	enjoys, causes to enjoy, undergoes, passes through,
dehapātāt	from the decay of the body, from death,
anantara	after, afterwards,

38. The *Karmakāṇḍa* also states that the Self is different from the body. After the death of the body it remains eternal and experiences the consequences of previous actions.

लिंगं चानेकसंयुक्तं चलं दृश्यं विकारि च ।
अव्यापकमसद्रूपं तत् कथं स्यात् पुमानयम् ।।३९।।

liṅgaṁ cānekasaṁyuktaṁ calaṁ dṛśyaṁ vikāri ca

avyāpakamasadrūpaṁ tat kathaṁ syāt pumānayam

liṅgam	the invariable mark which proves the existence of anything in an object, a mark, sign, anything having an origin and therefore liable to destruction, the subtle body (V),
ca	and
aneka	not one, many, much
-saṁyuktam	joined together, united, combined,
calam	unsteady, fluctuating, perishable, confused,
dṛśyam	visible, conspicuous, to be looked at, worth seeing, any visible object,
vikāri	changes,
ca	and
avyāpakam	peculiar, not spread over or pervading the whole, not an invariable concomitant, special,
asat	unreal, non-existent,
-rūpam	form, shape, figure, nature, of non-existent nature,
tat	that
katham	how
syāt	it could be, it should be,
pumān	the Puruṣa,
ayam	this,

39. The subtle body is made of many parts, unsteady, an object of perception, subject to change, limited and without true reality. How could it be this *Puruṣa*?

एवं देहद्वयादन्य आत्मा पुरुष ईश्वरः ।
सर्वात्मा सर्वरूपश्च सर्वातीतोऽहमव्ययः ।।४०।।

evam dehadvayādanya ātmā puruṣa īśvaraḥ
sarvātmā sarvarūpaḥ ca sarvātīto' hamavyayaḥ

evam	thus
deha-dvayāt	from two bodies,
anya	other, another, other than, different,
ātmā	the Self,
puruṣa	Puruṣa,
īśvara,	Īṣvara,
sarvātmā	the Self of all,
sarvarūpaḥ	assuming all forms,
ca	and,
sarvātītaḥ	who is beyond all,
aham	I,
avyayaḥ	indestructible, not liable to change,

40. Thus, different from the physical and subtle body is the Self, the *Puruṣa* or *Īṣvara.* I am the Self of all, assuming all forms, transcending all, indestructible and unchangeable.

इत्यात्मदेहभागेन प्रपञ्चस्यैव सत्यता ।
यथोक्ता तर्कशास्त्रेण ततः किं पुरुषार्थता ॥४१॥

ityātmadehabhāgena prapañcasyaiva satyatā
yathoktā tarkaśāstreṇa tataḥ kiṁ puruṣārthatā

iti	thus
ātma	from the Self
-deha	of the body
-bhāgena	with/by share or division, 3/s,
-prapañcasya	manifestation, manifoldness, 6/s of that
eva	very, indeed,
satyatā	truth, reality,
yathā	as
uktā	said, spoken,
tarkaśāstreṇa	3/s by the expositions on dialectics, science, reasoning and debate,
tataḥ	so
kiṁ	what,
puruṣārtha	objects of human pursuit, one of the four objects or aims of human life

41. Thus division of the Self from the body is comparable to the separation of truth or reality from the manifest (as asserted by the *tarkaśāstra*). How does this relate to the pursuit of the objects of life?

इत्यात्मदेहभेदेन देहात्मत्वं निवारितं ।
इदानीं देहभेदस्य ह्यसत्त्वं स्फुटमुच्यते ।।४२।।

ityātmadehabhedena dehātmatvaṁ nivāritaṁ
idānīṁ dehabhedasya hyasattvaṁ sphuṭamucyate

iti	thus
ātma	from the Self
-deha	of the body
-bhedena	by/with the difference, (by the difference between the body and the Self)
deha	of the body
-ātmatvam	the essence or nature 2/s,
nivāritam	prevented, deterred, kept off, hindered, prohibited, 2/s
idānīm	at the present time, now, soon,
dehabhedasya	the difference of the body (from the ātman),
hi	for, because, on account of,
asattvam	strengthless, without energy, non-presence, absence, 2/s,
sphuṭam	true, real, clear,
ucyate	it is said,

42. Thus, by the difference between the body and the Self the nature of the body (as the Self) is denied. Now it is said that the difference between them is because without the *ātman* the body is lifeless.

⧈

चैतन्यस्यैकरूपत्वाद्भेदो युक्तो न कर्हिचित् ।
जीवत्वं च मृषा ज्ञेयं रज्जौ सर्पग्रहो यथा ॥

caitanyasyaikarūpatvādbhedo yukto na karhicit
jīvatvaṁ ca mṛṣā jñeyaṁ rajjau sarpagraho yathā

caitanyasya	of consciousness 6/s
eka	one, only, alone,
-rūpatvāt	from the state of having form, figure, shape, nature,
bhedaḥ	breaking, splitting, cleaving, division, difference, interruption,
yuktaḥ	joined, fastened, attached, engaged in, combined,
na	not,
karhicit	at any time,
jīvatvam	the state of life, the state of the individual soul
ca	and,
mṛṣā	in vain, uselessly, to no purpose, wrongly, (with *jñā* to consider false or untrue),
jñeyam	to be learnt or understood, or perceived or investigated,
rajjau	in a/the rope 7/s,
sarpagrahaḥ	the perception of a snake,
yathā	as, like,

43. Interruption of the nature of the engagement in the unity of consciousness is not possible at any time. The individuality of the soul is to be understood as false like the perception of a snake in a rope.

◘

रज्ज्वज्ञानात् क्षणेनैव यद्वद्रज्जुर्हि सर्पिणी ।
भाति तद्वच्चितिः साक्षाद्विश्वाकारेण केवला ।।४४।।

rajjvajñānāt kṣaṇenaiva yadvadrajjurhi sarpiṇī
bhāti tadvaccitiḥ sākṣādviśvākāreṇa kevalā

rajju	a, the rope,
ajñānāt	through ignorance, non-cognizance,
kṣaṇena	instant, moment, twinkling of an eye 3/s,
eva	indeed, very,
yadvat	just as,
rajjuḥ	a/the rope,
hi	because, for, since, on account of,
sarpiṇī	the snake f.
bhāti	it shines, light, splendour, evidence, perception, knowledge, appears as,
tadvat	so, thus,
citiḥ	understanding,
sākṣāt	from/through the witness, visibly, direct, before one's eyes, realize, with one's own eyes,
viśvākāreṇa	by/with having the form of the universe,
kevalā	alone, only, mere, sole, one,

44. Just as a rope not recognized as a rope may, in an instant, be seen as a snake similarly the One alone is seen before one's eyes in the form of the universe.

उपादानं प्रपञ्चस्य ब्रह्मणोऽन्यन्न विद्यते ।
तस्मात् सर्वप्रपञ्चोऽयं ब्रह्मैवास्ति न चेतरत् ॥४५॥

upādānaṁ prapañcasya brahmaṇo'nyanna vidyate
tasmāt sarvaprapañco'yaṁ brahmaivāsti na cetarat

upādānam	taking to one-self, perceiving, noticing, learning, acquiring, material, cause, material cause,
prapañcasya	manifestation, manifoldness, 6/s of that ,
brahmaṇaḥ	6/s of the Brahman,
anyat	other, another,
na	not,
vidyate	is seen, there exists, there is, is
tasmāt	from that,
sarvaprapañcaḥ	manifestation of all, manifoldness of all,
ayam	this,
brahma	the Brahman
eva	indeed,
asti	is,
na	not,
ca	and,
itarat(as)	different from, otherwise than,

45. This Brahman is indeed not other than the manifestation of the universe. The Brahman is the material cause of it and there is nothing else.

□

व्याप्यव्यापकता मिथ्या सर्वमात्मैति शासनात् ।
इति ज्ञाते परे तत्त्वे भेदस्यावसरः कुतः ॥४६॥

vyāpyavyāpakatā mithyā sarvamātmaiti śāsanāt
iti jñāte pare tattve bhedasyāvasaraḥ kutaḥ

vyāpi	reaching through, pervading, diffusive, spreading everywhere, pervader, an invariably pervading property as characteristic,
avyāpakatā	f. non-comprehensiveness or generalization, speciality,
mithyā	not real, neither real not unreal, illusory,
sarvam	completely, everything, all,
ātmā	the Self,
iti	end of quote,
śāsanāt	punishing, a punisher, teaching, instructing, an instructor, instruction, doctrine, a work of authority, 5/s from *śruti,*
iti	end of quote,
jñāte	known , ascertained, comprehended, understood, taken for, known as, 7/s
pare	far, distant, remote, other than, different from, supreme, 7/s,
tattve	true or real state, truth, reality, 7/s,
bhedasya	breaking, splitting, cleaving, schism, change, alteration, 6/s
avasaraḥ	occasion, moment, favourable opportunity, anyone's turn, appropriate place for anything, advantageous situation, 1/s
kutaḥ	from whence, from whom, how?

46. "All this is the Self", is a statement with the authority of *śruti* so it follows that pervasiveness as a quality of the Self is illusory. In the light of this supreme knowledge of truth what is the cause of change, alteration or difference? (Or where is any opportunity or point of distinction between the Self and it's manifestation).

श्रुत्या निवारितं नूनं नानात्वं स्वमुखेन हि ।

कथं भासो भवेदन्यः स्थिते चाद्वयकारणे ।।४७।।

śrutyā nivāritaṁ nūnaṁ nānātvaṁ svamukhena hi

kathaṁ bhāso bhavedanyaḥ sthite cādvayakāraṇe

śrutyā	by the *śruti*,
nivāritam	kept off, hindered, prevented, prohibited, denied,
nūnam	indeed, at present, now, immediately, certainly,
nānātvam	difference, manifoldness, variety,
svamukhena	by own mouth,
hi	for, since, because,
katham	how?
bhāsaḥ	light, brightness, lustre,
bhavet	it could be, it should be,
anyaḥ	other, another,
sthite	*7/s* in abiding by, standing, remaining, intent upon,
ca	and,
advayakāraṇe	7/s in non-dual cause or reason,

47. Certainly variation of Brahman is denied by *śruti* itself, since how could that light be 'other' while steady in non-dual causality. i.e. the non-dual cause having been established then how could the manifestation be different from that cause?

दोषोऽपि श्रुत्या मृत्योर्मृत्युं स गच्छति ।
इह पश्यति नानात्वं मायया वञ्चितो नरः ।।४८।।

doṣo'pi śrutyā mṛtyormṛtyuṁ sa gacchati
iha paśyati nānātvaṁ māyayā vañcito naraḥ

doṣaḥ	fault, want, deficiency, reproach,
api	also
śrutyā	by *ṣruti* 3/s
mṛtyoḥ-mṛtyuṁ	from death to death,
saḥ	he
gacchati	he goes,
iha	here, in this place, in this world,
paśyati	he sees
nānātvaṁ	difference, variety, manifoldness,
māyayā	by or through illusion,
vañcitaḥ	deceived, tricked, imposed, a kind of riddle or enigma,
naraḥ	a man, man, a person,

48. A person seeing difference in this world is tricked by the illusion of *māyā. Śruti* states that a person with this disadvantage goes from death to death.

◘

ब्रह्मणः सर्वभूतानि जयन्ते परमात्मनः ।
तस्मादेतानि ब्रह्मैव भवन्तित्यवधारयेत् ॥४९॥

brahmaṇaḥ sarvabhūtāni jayante paramātmanaḥ
tasmādetāni brahmaiva bhavantītyavadhārayet

brahmaṇaḥ	from the Brahman 5/s
sarvabhūtāni	all beings,
jayante	are born,
paramātmanaḥ	the Self,
tasmāt	from that, therefore,
etāni	they, (pron.),
brahma	the Brahman
eva indeed,	only alone,
bhavanti	he becomes,
iti	end of quote,
avadhārayet	he should understand, determine, affirm, ascertain,

49. All beings originate from Brahman therefore they indeed are the Supreme Self. One should come to understand this.

ब्रह्मैव सर्वनामानि रूपाणि विविधानि च ।
कर्माण्यपि समग्राणि विभर्तीति श्रुतिर्जगौ ।।५०।।

brahmaiva sarvanāmāni rūpāṇi vividhāni ca
karmāṇyapi samagrāṇi vibhartīti śrutirjagau

brahma	Brahman,
eva	indeed, verily,
sarvanāmāni	names of all,
rūpāṇi	forms,
vividhāni	of various sorts, manifold, variously,
ca	and,
karmāṇi	actions,
api	also,
samagrāṇi	all, entire, whole, complete, each, fully provided with,
vibharti	he/it spreads out, spreads asunder,
iti	end of quote,
śrutiḥ	*śruti*,
jagau	he/it sang, said, taught, instructed, 1/s/perf./√*gai* Cl.2

50. The śruti has taught that "Brahman is indeed everything. He spreads out completely as all variations of names, forms and actions."
or " … as the substratum of all variations of names, forms and actions."

सुवर्णाज्जायमानस्य सुवर्णत्वं च शाश्वतम् ।
ब्रह्मणो जायमानस्य ब्रह्मत्वं च भवेत, ।।५१।।

suvarṇājjāyamānasya suvarṇatvaṁ ca śāśvatam
brahmaṇo jāyamānasya brahmatvaṁ ca bhavet

suvarṇāt	5/s from gold
jāyamānasya	6/s a thing produced or born of (pres.part. *jan),*
suvarṇatvam	having the nature of gold,
ca	and
śāśvatam	evermore, eternal,
brahmaṇaḥ	5/6/s of/from Brahman
jāyamānasya	6/s produced or born of,
brahmatvam	having the nature of Brahman
ca	and
bhavet	may it be,

51. Just as something made from gold has the nature of gold;
so it is that anything produced from Brahman ever has the nature of Brahman.

स्वल्पमप्यन्तरं कृत्वा जीवात्मपरमात्मनोः ।
यः संतिष्ठति मूढात्मा भयं तस्याभिभाषितम् ।।५२।।

svalpamapyantaraṁ kṛtvā jīvātmaparamātmanoḥ
yaḥ saṁtiṣṭhati mūḍhātmā bhayaṁ tasyābhibhāṣitam

svalpam	very small or little, minute, very few,
api	also, surely, even, very,
antaram	in the interior, interior, proximate, intimate, related, adjacent to, different from,
kṛtvā	having made, done, performed,
jīvātma	(the individual Self)
-paramātmanoḥ	(the Supreme Self) 6/7/du. of or in, between the individual Self and the Brahman,
yaḥ	who
saṁtiṣṭhati	holds together, remains, stands together, abides,
mūḍha	stupid, foolish, a fool,
-ātmā	the Self, the self,
bhayam	fear, apprehension,
tasya	of him, of that,
abhibhāṣitam	addressed, spoken to, spoken of, n.pl. word,

52. It is said that he who finds even tiny differences between the Jīvātman and the Supreme Ātman remains foolish, fearful of the Self.

यत्राज्ञानाद्भवेद्द्वैतमितरस्तत्र पश्यति ।
आत्मत्वेन यदा सर्वं नेतरस्तत्र चाण्वपि ।।५३।।

yatrājñānādbhaveddvaitamitarastatra paśyati
ātmatvena yadā sarvaṁ netarastatra cāṇvapi

yatra	when
ajñānāt	through ignorance 5/s
bhavet	it might, should become,
dvaitam	dual, duality,
itaras	the other (of two), another,
tatra	then,
paśyati	sees
ātmatvena	by one, by one-self, through one-self,
yadā	when,
sarvam	all,
na	not
itaras	the other (of two), another,
tatra	then,
ca	and,
aṇvapi	even a little

53. When through ignorance duality arises then one sees another. When all is seen as one-self then there is not even the slightest perception of other.

◻

यस्मिन् सर्वाणि भूतानि ह्यात्मत्वेन विजानतः ।
न वै तस्य भवेन्मोहो न च शोकोऽद्वितीयतः ।।५४।।

yasmin sarvāṇi bhūtāṇi hyātmatvena vijānataḥ
na vai tasya bhavenmoho na ca śoko'dvitīyataḥ

yasmin	when
sarvāṇi	all,
bhūtāṇi	beings,
hi	for, since, because, on account of,
ātmatvena	with (having) the nature of the Self
vijānataḥ	(6/s of) having understood, known or realized,
na	not,
vai	indeed,
tasya	of that,
bhavet	it should,could, might, be,
mohaḥ	dullness, delusion,
na	not,
ca	and,
śokaḥ	grief, sorrow,
advitīyataḥ	in the absence of duality,

54. When all beings are as one self through self-realization and duality is absent then delusion and sorrow do not arise.

अयमात्मा हि ब्रह्मैव सर्वात्मकतया स्थितः ।
इति निर्धारितं श्रुत्या बृहदारण्यसंस्थया ।।५५।।

ayamātmā hi brahmaiva sarvātmakatayā sthitaḥ
iti nirdhāritaṁ śrutyā bṛhadāraṇyasaṁsthayā

ayam	this
ātmā	Self,
hi	for, since, because, on account of,
brahma	Brahman
eva	indeed, verily,
sarva	of all 5/s,
ātmakatayā	having or consisting of the nature or character of, 3/s by, with, through, as the Self of all,
sthitaḥ	present, existing, established, being there,
iti	end of quote,
nirdhāritam	settled, determined, ascertained, accurately stated or told,
śrutyā	by the *śruti* ,
bṛhadāraṇyasaṁsthayā	established in the Bṛhadāraṇyakopaniṣada

55. "This Ātman (the Self) is indeed the present, existent Brahman, the Self of all." This has been definitively stated by *śruti* in the Bṛhadāraṇyaka Upaniṣad (2/5/19)

अनुभूतोऽप्ययं लोको व्यवहारक्षमोऽपि सन् ।
असद्रूपो यथा स्वप्न उत्तरक्षणबाधतः ।।५६।।

anubhūto'pyayaṁ loko vyavahārakṣamo'pi san
asadrūpo yathā svapna uttarakṣaṇabādhataḥ

anubhūtaḥ	perceived, understood, apprehended, experienced,
api	even, also,
ayam	this,
lokaḥ	world,
vyavahāra	common practice or usage, doing, performing, conduct, behaviour,
-kṣamaḥ	competent, able, fit for, (able practically),
api	also, even,
san	1/s/m *sat* being, existing,
asat	non-existent, unreal,
rūpaḥ	form, shape, figure,
yathā	as like,
svapna	dream, sleep,
uttara	later, consequent,
-kṣaṇa	a point in time, instant, moment,
-bādhataḥ	contradicted, objected to, absurdity, (contradicted at a subsequent point in time),

56. This world is practically experienced by us in every-day life but the forms experienced can be considered as being dream-like, unreal or non-existent, in that whatever is experienced is subject to contradiction next moment.

स्वप्नो जागरणेऽलीक स्वप्नेऽपि जागरो न हि ।
द्वयमेव लये नास्ति लयोऽपि ह्युभयोर्न च ।।५७।।

svapno jāgaraṇe'līka svapne'pi jāgaro na hi
dvayameva laye nāsti layo'pi hyubhayorna ca

svapnaḥ	dream 1/s
jāgaraṇe	7/s mfn awake, on waking, keeping watch,
alīka	mfn unpleasing, disagreeable, untrue, false, pretended, n. anything displeasing, falsehood, untruth,
svapne	7/s in dream,
api	also, whereas
jāgaraḥ	1/s mfn awake, in waking, keeping watch,
na	not
hi	ind. for, since, because,
dvayam	mfn double, of 2 kinds or sorts, n. couple, pair, twofold nature,
eva	indeed, only,
laye	7/s m. the act of sticking or clinging to, lying down, melting, dissolution, disappearance or absorption in, extinction,
na asti	not is
layaḥ	1/s m. the act of sticking or clinging to, lying down, melting, dissolution, disappearance or absorption in, extinction,
api	also
hi	for, since, because
ubhayoḥ	6/7/ du. *ubhaya* of both kinds, in both ways,
na ca	not and

57. A dream is found to be unreal on waking and awakeness is absent in dream. Neither of these experiences exist in deep sleep for experiencing is not possible while the mind is absorbed (in the Self and consequently inactive) .

त्रयमेवं भवेन्मिथ्या गुणत्रयविनिर्मितम् ।

अस्य द्रष्टा गुणातीतो नित्यो ह्येकश्चिदात्मकः ।।५८।।

trayamevaṁ bhavenmithyā guṇatrayavinirmitam

asya draṣṭā guṇātīto nityo hyekaścidātmakaḥ

trayam	2/s consisting of three, of 3 kinds, a triad
evam	thus, in this way,
bhavet	1/s/opt/act it should be or become, it may be
mithyā	ind. incorrectly, wrongly, falsely, not in reality, only apparently,
guṇatraya	by the 3 guṇā (TP comp. with below)
vinirmitam	mfn formed, created, made, 2/s
asya	of that, of this,
draṣṭā	f. the seer, the pure consciousness comprehending all objects,
guṇā	the *guṇā* pl.
atītaḥ	mfn one who has gone through or over or beyond,
nityaḥ	1/s eternal,
hi	for, since, because, indeed,
ekaḥ	1/s one
cidātmakaḥ	mfn consisting of pure thought, having the nature of consciousness,

58. Thus though the three states (waking, dreaming and deep sleep) may be created by the three *guṇā* the reality of all of them is only apparent. The seer of this, the one pure consciousness comprehending all objects, is beyond the *guṇā,* eternal, and indeed, one.

◘

यद्वन्मृदि घटभ्रान्तिं शुक्तौ वा रजतस्थितिम् ।

तद्वद्ब्रह्मणि जीवत्वं विक्षमाणे न पश्यति ।।५९।।

yadvanmṛdi ghaṭabhrāntiṁ śuktau vā rajatasthitim

tadvadbrahmaṇi jīvatvaṁ vikṣamāṇe na paśyati

yadvat ind. in which way, just as

mṛdi *mṛd* f. earth, soil, 7/s in earth,

ghaṭabhrāntiṁ *ghaṭa* m. a jar, pitcher, jug,

-bhrāntiṁ 2/s perplexity, doubt, false opinion, mistaking something for,

śuktau 7/s in *śukti* pearl-shell, nacre,

vā or

rajatasthitim *rajata* mfn silver

-sthitim 2/s f. position, stay, presence, existence of silver

tadvat so

brahmaṇi 7/s in Brahman

jīva the *Jīva*

tvam you

vikṣamāṇe √*vīkṣ* to see, behold, look at, observe, discern, understand, 7/s pres.part. in understanding, knowing, realizing,

na not

paśyati he sees

59. In the same way as one does not see an earthen jar in earth , or mistake a pearl shell for the presence of silver so one who has realised does not see the Jīva in Brahman.

⊡

यथा मृदि घटो नाम कनके कुण्डलाभिधा ।

शुक्तौ हि रजतख्यातिर्जीवशब्दस्तथा परे ॥६०॥

yathā mṛdi ghaṭo nāma kanake kuṇḍalābhidhā

śuktau hi rajatakhyātirjīvaśabdastathā pare

yathā as, like

mṛdi 7/s/f *mṛdā* in earth

ghaṭaḥ a pitcher, jug

nāma named, called

kanake *7/s kanaka* in gold,

kuṇḍalābhidhā

kuṇḍalā n. a ring, ear-ring, bracelet, a fetter, tie,

abhidhā f. the literal power or sense of a word, name, a word, sound,

śuktau 7/s in *śukti* pearl-shell, nacre,

hi ind. as, for, since, because,

rajatakhyātirjīvaśabdastathā

rajata mfn silver-coloured, silvery, n. silver

khyātiḥ f. declaration, opinion, idea, assertion, renown, fame,

jīva the *Jīva*

śabdaḥ 1/s/ word, sound,

tathā so

pare 7/s *para* mfn in other, another, chief, supreme, remote,

60. As earth may nominally be called a jug, gold nominally a bracelet or pearl-shell named as silver, so in word alone the Jīva is nominally in the Supreme (Brahman).

यथैव व्योम्नि नीलत्वं यथा नीरं मरुस्थले ।

पुरुषत्वं यथा स्थाणौ तद्वद्विश्वं चिदात्मनि ॥६१॥

yathaiva vyomni nīlatvaṁ yathā nīraṁ marusthale
puruṣatvaṁ yathā sthāṇau tadvadviśvaṁ cidātmani

yathā	as, like,
eva	indeed, only
vyomni	7/s *vyoman* in sky
nīlatvaṁ	blueness
yathā	so
nīraṁ	2/s *nīra* juice, water,
marusthale	7/s in dry soil,
puruṣatvam	manhood, manliness, having the qualities of a man, 2/s
yathā	so
sthāṇau	7/s in a place, site, venue, form, act of standing, something fixed or stationary like a post,
tadvat	so
viśvaṁ	all, everything, the universe,
cidātmani	7/s in the conscious Self,

61. As the sky appears to be blue, water is seen as a mirage in the desert, or a post looks like a man, so the universe existing in the conscious Self is an appearance.

Note: It must be illusory or there would be duality. The reality is it is all One.

यथैव शून्ये वेतालो गन्धर्वाणां पुरं यथा ।

यथाकाशे द्विचन्द्रत्वं तद्वत् सत्ये जगत्स्थितिः ॥६२॥

yathaiva śūnye vetālo gandharvāṇāṁ puraṁ yathā

yathākāśe dvicandratvaṁ tadvat satye jagatsthitiḥ

yathā	as, like,
eva	indeed, verily,
śūnye	*śūnya* 7/s/mfn in empty, void, hollow, barren, deserted,
vetālaḥ	1/s a kind of demon, ghost, spirit, goblin,
gandharvāṇām	6/pl of the Gandharvans, of the heavenly musicians, among the Gandharvans (a celestial race)
puram	2/s a fortress, castle, city,
yathā	as, like,
yathā	as, like
-ākāśe	7/s in space, in the sky
dvicandratvam	having the form of two moons
tadvat	in the same way, similarly
satye	7/s *satya* mfn in true, real, actual, n. truth, reality,
jagatsthitiḥ	*jagat* the world, universe,
-sthitiḥ	f. standing upright or firmly, staying or remaining or being in any state or condition, continued existence,

62. Like a ghost in emptiness or an imagined castle in the heavens or two moons in the sky so in truth the existence of the universe in the Brahman is illusory.

Note: It must be illusory or there would be duality. The reality is it is all One.

यथा तरंगकल्लोलैर्जलमेव स्फुरत्यलम् ।

पात्ररूपेण ताम्रं हि ब्रह्माण्डौधैस्तथात्मता ।।६३।।

yathā taraṁgakallolairjalameva sphuratyalam

pātrarūpeṇa tāmraṁ hi brahmāṇḍaudhaistathātmatā

yathā as

taraṁgakallolaiḥ 3/pl *taraṁga* m. wave, billow, moving to and fro,

-kallola full of waves, huge wave, surge

jalam n. water

eva indeed, only, alone,

sphurati becomes evident or manifest, starts into view, springs out

alam mfn fitting, ready, ind. equal to, sufficient, adequate, competent,

pātrarūpeṇa *pātra* n. pot, can, tin, vessel

-rūpeṇa 3/s/n with the form or shape

tāmaṁ 2/s copper

hi for, since, because,

brahmāṇḍaudhais 3/pl *brahmāṇḍa* n. *Brahmā's* egg, the universe, the world,

-audhais /odhas/ūdhas relating to any udder, breast,

bosom as full (of milk),

tathā so

ātmatā f. essence, nature, the quality of being the Self,

63. Just like water appears in the form of waves and billows, or copper appears as a pot, so it is that the nature of the Self appears as the fullness of the universe.

◻

घटनाम्ना पृथ्वी यथा पटनाम्ना हि तंतवः ।

जगन्नाम्ना चिदाभाति ज्ञेयं तत्तदभावतः ॥६४॥

ghaṭanāmnā pṛthvī yathā paṭanāmnā hi taṁtavaḥ

jagannāmnā cidābhāti jñeyaṁ tattadabhāvataḥ

ghaṭanāmnā	*ghaṭa* a pitcher, jug
-nāmnā	by name
pṛthvī	earth
yathā	as,
paṭanāmnā	a piece of cloth by name
hi	for, since, indeed, because,
taṁtavaḥ	*ta(ā)ntava* mfn made of threads,
jagannāmnā	the universe by name
cidābhāti	*cid* consciousness, the conscious Self
-ābhāti	1/s/pres/act *ā√bhā* looks like, blazes towards, appears, shines, becomes visible or apparent,
jñeyam	2/s to be known, to be learnt or understood or perceived,
tat	that
tadabhāvataḥ	*tat* of those, of these
abhāvataḥ	*abhāva* ppp. 1/s/m non-existence, nullity, absence, non-entity, negation, negation of those (names)

64. As earth may be known by the name jar or a cloth called a cloth because it is made of threads, so also the universe is known through its name. All this is the appearance of the conscious Self . That (Ātman) is to be known through the negation of names.

⊡

सर्वोऽपि व्यवहारस्तु ब्रह्मणा क्रियते जनैः ।
अज्ञानान्न विजानन्ति मृदेव हि घटादिकम् ।।६५।।

sarvo'pi vyavahārastu brahmaṇā kriyate janaiḥ
ajñānānna vijānanti mṛdeva hi ghaṭādikam

sarvaḥ	all
api	also
vyavahārastu	7/pl m. doing, performing, action, practice, conduct, behaviour, affair, matter, custom, usage, common practice,
brahmaṇā	3/s by/with/through *Brahman*
kriyate	1/s/pass/ √*kṛ* it is done made, performed
janaiḥ	3/pl by/with the people,
ajñānān	2/pl non-cognizance, ignorance, spiritual ignorance,
na	not
vijānanti	*(vijānānti ?)* 1/pl/act/pres *vi*√*jñā* they distinguish, discern, observe, ascertain, know, understand,
mṛt	earth, soil, clay,
eva	indeed, only, alone, verily,
hi	for, since, because,
ghaṭa	jug, pitcher, jar
ādikam	2/s beginning with

65. Also all everyday actions are performed by people through Brahman but because of ignorance they are not aware of this just as they are not aware that jugs and other such are just forms of earth.

कार्यकारणता नित्यमास्ते घटमृदोर्यथा ।
तथैव श्रुतियुक्तिभ्यां प्रपञ्चब्रह्मणोरिह ।।६६।।

kāryakāraṇatā nityamāste ghaṭamṛdoryathā
tathaiva śrutiyuktibhyāṁ prapañcabrahmaṇoriha

kāryakāraṇatā *kārya* mfn to be made, done or practised or performed,
n. an effect, result,
-kāraṇatā f. causality, causation, cause and effect
nityam mfn continual, perpetual, eternal,
āste 1/s/pres/mid √*ās* exists, is present,
ghaṭamṛdoryathā *ghaṭa* jug, pitcher, jar
-mṛdoḥ 6/7/du/f *mṛd* of or from earth, soil, clay
a jug from clay
yathā as *tatha* so *eva* indeed
śrutiyuktibhyāṁ *śruti* revealed sacred texts
yuktibhyāṁ 3/du/f union, junction, connection, application,
practice, reasoning, argument, deduction,
connection of events through *śruti* and reason
prapañcabrahmaṇoriha *prapañca* m. expansion, development, manifestation,
manifoldness, diversity, appearance, phenomenon,
brahmaṇoḥ 6/7/du/ of /from *Brahman,*
from *Brahman* and the phenomenal world,
iha ind. in this place, here, in this world, now, at this time,

66. Cause and effect are ever present. Just as indeed a jug comes from clay so through revealed scripture and through reason it may be seen that the phenomenal world relates to Brahman in the same way in every moment.

◻

गृह्यमाणे घटे यद्वन्मृत्तिकाऽयाति वै बलात् ।
वीक्षमाणे प्रपञ्चऽपि ब्रह्मैवाभाति भासुरम् ॥६७॥

gṛhyamāṇe ghaṭe yadvanmṛttikā'yāti vai balāt
vīkṣamāṇe prapañca'pi brahmaivābhāti bhāsuram

gṛhyamāṇe 7/s, pres.part. of *gṛhya* in perceiving, to be acknowledged or admitted, in acknowledging,

ghaṭe 7/s pot, jug, vessel

yadvanmṛttikā'yāti *yadvat* ind. in which way,

-*mṛttikāḥ* f. earth, clay, loam,

āyāti *ā√yā* 1/s/pres coming from, is coming, comes,

vai indeed

balāt 5/s/n from power, stamina, force,

vīkṣamāṇe 7/s pres.part. *vīkṣa* m. sight, seeing,

prapañcaḥ m. expansion, development, manifestation, manifoldness, diversity, appearance, phenomenon,

api also

brahmaivābhāti *brahma* *Brahman*

-*eva* indeed, only, alone,

-*ābhāti* 1/s/pres/act *ā√bhā* becomes visible or apparent, looks like, shines or blazes towards, illumines, shines,

bhāsuram 2/s mfn terrible, splendid, bright, radiant, distinguished by,

67. As (one) comes back from the force of seeing and acknowledges a seen pot to be clay; so, in the same way the Brahman alone shining forth becomes apparent.

⊡

सदैवात्मा विशुद्धोऽस्ति ह्यशुद्धो भाति वै सदा ।

यथैव द्विविधा रज्जुर्ज्ञानिनोऽज्ञानिनोऽनिशम् ॥६८॥

sadaivātmā viśuddho'sti hyaśuddho bhāti vai sadā

yathaiva dvividhā rajjurjñānino'jñānino'niśam

sadaivātmā *sadaiva* ind. always, ever,

-ātmā the Self 1/s/m

viśuddho'sti *viśuddhaḥ* mfn very pure, thoroughly settled, free from vice, completely cleansed or purified,

-asti is

hyaśuddho *hi* for, since, because,

-aśuddhaḥ impure 1/s/m

bhāti 1/s/pres/act√*bhā* it shines, exists, manifests, appears

vai indeed,

sadā ind. eternally, ever, always, perpetually,

yathaiva just as

dvividhā ind. in two ways, mfn of two kinds, twofold,

rajjurjñānino'jñānino'niśam *rajjuḥ* 1/s rope

- jñāninaḥ 5/6/s of/from *jñānin* endowed with knowledge or intelligence, knowing, knowing the higher knowledge, wise,

-ajñāninaḥ 5/6/s of or from the unwise, not wise

aniśam ind. continually, always,

68. The Self is always completely pure to the wise and impure to the unwise. Just as a rope may be seen as a rope by those who know, or seen as a snake by those who do not.

यथैव मृन्मयः कुम्भस्तद्वद्देहोऽपि चिन्मयः ।

आत्मानात्मविभागोऽयं मुधैव क्रियतेऽबुधैः ।।६९।।

yathaiva mṛnmayaḥ kumbhastadvaddeho'pi cinmayaḥ

ātmānātmavibhāgo'yaṁ mudhaiva kriyate'budhaiḥ

yathaiva just as

mṛnmayaḥ made of or consisting of earth or clay, earthen,

kumbhastadvaddeho'pi *kumbhaḥ* 1/s/m pitcher, jar, water-pot,

-tadvat ind. in the same way

-dehaḥ api the body also

cinmayaḥ 1/s/m consisting of pure consciousness

ātmānātmavibhāgo'yaṁ *ātmā* 1/s/m the Self

-anātma the not-Self

-vibhāgaḥ partition, apportionment, division,

ayam this

mudha ind. uselessly, wrongly, falsely, in vain,

eva indeed, verily, only

kriyate'budhaiḥ *kriyate* 1/s/pass/*kṛ* is made, done, performed,

-abudhaiḥ 3/pl/m. fool mfn stupid, by the foolish,

69. Just as a water-pot is made from clay, in the same way the body consists of pure consciousness alone. Therefore this division into the Self and the not-Self is a fruitless exercise performed by those who do not understand this.

◻

सर्पत्वेन यथा रज्जु रजतत्वे शुक्तिका ।
विनिर्णीता विमूढेन देहत्वेन तथात्मता ॥७०॥

sarpatvena yathā rajju rajatatvena śuktikā
vinirṇītā vimūḍhena dehatvena tathātmatā

sarpatvena	with the nature of a snake
yathā	as, like
rajjuḥ	a rope
rajatatvena	with the appearance of silver
śuktikā	mother of pearl,
vinirṇītā	mfn determined clearly, certain, ascertained,
vimūḍhena	m. by a foolish or confused person
dehatvena	with the characteristics of a body
tathā	so
ātmatā	f. nature, essence, the nature of the Self,

70. As a rope is considered to be a snake or mother-of-pearl appears to be silver, so to an ignorant person, the Self may seem to be the body.

घटत्वेन यथा पृथ्वी पटत्वेनैव तन्तवः ।

विनिर्णीता विमूढेन देहत्वेन तथात्मता ।।७१।।

ghaṭatvena yathā pṛthvī paṭatvenaiva tantavaḥ

vinirṇītā vimūḍhena dehatvena tathātmatā

ghaṭatvena	with the characteristics of a pot
yathā	as
pṛthvī	earth, the element earth,
paṭatvena	with the characteristics of cloth
eva	indeed, only,
tantavaḥ	mfn made of threads, fabric,
vinirṇītā	mfn determined clearly, certain, ascertained,
vimūḍhena	m. by a foolish or confused person
dehatvena	with the characteristics of a body
tathā	so
ātmatā	f. nature, essence, the nature of the Self,

71. As earth has commonality with an earthen pot or something made of threads is considered to be cloth, so to an ignorant person, the Self may seem to be the body.

कनकं कुण्डलत्वेन तरङ्गत्वेन वै जलम् ।
विनिर्णीता विमूढेन देहत्वेन तथात्मता ॥७२॥

kanakaṁ kuṇḍalatvena taraṅgatvena vai jalam
vinirṇītā vimūḍhena dehatvena tathātmatā

kanakam	gold
kuṇḍalatvena	having the characteristics of a bracelet,
taraṅgatvena	having the characteristics of waves
vai	emphasis
jalam	water
vinirṇītā	mfn determined clearly, certain, ascertained,
vimūḍhena	m. by a foolish or confused person
dehatvena	with the characteristics of a body
tathā	so
ātmatā	f. nature, essence, the nature of the Self,

72. As gold may have the characteristics of a bracelet or water is seen as a wave so to an ignorant person, the Self may seem to be the body.

पुरुषत्वेन वै स्थाणुर्जलत्वेन मरीचिका ।
विनिर्णीता विमूढेन देहत्वेन तथात्मता ।।७३।।

puruṣatvena vai sthāṇurjalatvena marīcikā
vinirṇītā vimūḍhena dehatvena tathātmatā

puruṣatvena	having the appearance (characteristics) of a person
vai	indeed
sthāṇuḥ	a post or stump,
jalatvena	having the nature of water
marīcikā	mirage, appearance of water in the desert
vinirṇītā	mfn determined clearly, certain, ascertained,
vimūḍhena	m. by a foolish or confused person
dehatvena	with the characteristics of a body
tathā	so
ātmatā	f. nature, essence, the nature of the Self,

73. As a tree-stump may appear to be a person or a desert mirage may seem to be water so, the Self may seem to be the body to an ignorant person.

गृहत्वेनैव काष्ठानि खड्गत्वेनैव लोहता ।

विनिर्णीता विमूढेन देहत्वेन तथात्मता ।।७४।।

gṛhatvenaiva kāṣṭhāni khaṅgatvenaiva lohatā
vinirṇītā vimūḍhena dehatvena tathātmatā

gṛhatvena	by/with having the nature of a house
eva	indeed
kāṣṭhāni	pieces of timber
khaṅgatvena	by/with having the nature of a sword,
eva	indeed,
lohatā	*loha* m. iron
vinirṇītā	mfn determined clearly, certain, ascertained,
vimūḍhena	m. by a foolish or confused person
dehatvena	with the characteristics of a body
tathā	so
ātmatā	f. nature, essence, the nature of the Self,

74. As pieces of timber may seem to be a house or iron seems to be a sword, so to an ignorant person, the Self may seem to be the body.

⧈

यथा वृक्षविपर्यासो जलाद्भवति कस्यचित् ।

तद्वदात्मनि देहत्वं पश्यत्यज्ञानयोगतः ।।७५।।

yathā vṛkṣaviparyāso jalādbhavati kasyacit

tadvadātmani dehatvaṁ paśyatyajñānayogataḥ

yathā	as
vṛkṣa	tree
viparyāsaḥ	1/s /m opposite of, imagining what is unreal or false to be true, delusion, mistake,
jalāt	from water,
bhavati	it becomes, arises
kasyacit	of someone, to someone
tadvat	so, similarly
ātmani	7/s/m in the Self
dehatvam	2/s having the nature of the body
paśyati	he sees
ajñāna	n. ignorance, mfn unwise, of ignorance
yogataḥ	3/s by contact of, by means of, by contact with,

75. As a tree mistakenly seems to someone to be growing out of water so similarly through contact with ignorance he sees the Self as having the nature of the body.

▣

पोतेन गच्छतः पुंसः सर्वं भातीव चञ्चलं ।

तद्वदात्मनि देहत्वं पश्यत्यज्ञानयोगतः ॥७६॥

potena gacchataḥ puṁsaḥ sarvaṁ bhātīva cañcalaṁ
tadvadātmani dehatvaṁ paśyatyajñānayogataḥ

potena	m. a young animal or plant, cloth, a garment, a vessel, ship, boat, 3/s with a boat, (in a boat),
gacchataḥ	gone, going,
puṁsaḥ	5/6/s/m of, from a person
sarvam	all
bhātī	shines, appears,
iva	as if
cañcalam	f. lightning, mfn moving to and fro, unsteady, quivering,
tadvat	so, similarly
ātmani	7/s/m in the Self
dehatvam	2/s having the nature of the body
paśyati	he sees
ajñāna	n. ignorance, mfn unwise, of ignorance
yogataḥ	3/s by contact of, by means of, by contact with,

76. To a person travelling in a boat everything appears to be moving. Similarly a person in ignorance sees the Self as having the characteristics of the body.

पीतत्वं हि तथा शुभ्रे दोषाद्भवति कस्यचित् ।
तद्वदात्मनि देहत्वं पश्यत्यज्ञानयोगतः ॥७७॥

pītatvaṁ hi tathā śubhre doṣādbhavati kasyacit
tadvadātmani dehatvaṁ paśyatyajñānayogataḥ

pītatvam	yellowness
hi	ind. for, since, because,
tathā	as, like,
śubhre	7/s mfn in white (thing)
doṣāt	5/s mfn from, through, defect, blame,
bhavati	1/s/pres √*bhū* it becomes, appears,
kasyacit	ind. anyone's, for someone, of some, of someone,
tadvat	so, similarly
ātmani	7/s/m in the Self
dehatvam	2/s having the nature of the body
paśyati	he sees
ajñāna	n. ignorance, mfn unwise, of ignorance
yogataḥ	3/s by contact of, by means of, by contact with,

77. As yellowness may appear in something white because of a defect (like jaundice), so a person in ignorance sees the Self as having the characteristics of the body.

चक्षुर्भ्यां भ्रमशीलाभ्यां सर्वं भाति भ्रमात्मकं ।

तद्वदात्मनि देहत्वं पश्यत्यज्ञानयोगतः ॥७८॥

cakṣurbhyāṁ bhramaśīlābhyāṁ sarvaṁ bhāti bhramātmakaṁ

tadvadātmani dehatvaṁ paśyatyajñānayogataḥ

cakṣurbhyām	5/du/ through the eyes
bhramaśīlābhyām	2/du
bhrama	m. unsteadiness, error, mistake, confusion
-śīla	mfn practising, habituated, accustomed, accustomed to wrong or poor vision
sarvaṁ	all, everything,
bhāti	shines, appears, manifests, 1/s/pres/act √*bhā*
bhramātmakam	*bhrama* as above
-ātmakam	2/s suffix, consisting of, having or consisting of the nature or character of, has/having a defective nature
tadvat	so, similarly
ātmani	7/s/m in the Self
dehatvam	2/s having the nature of the body
paśyati	he sees
ajñāna	n. ignorance, mfn unwise, of ignorance
yogataḥ	3/s by contact of, by means of, by contact with,

78. As a person with defective vision sees everything distorted so a person in ignorance may see the Self as having the characteristics of the body.

अलातं भ्रमणेनैव वर्तुलं भाति सूर्यवत् ।

तद्वदात्मनि देहत्वं पश्यत्यज्ञानयोगतः ।।७९।।

alātaṁ bhramaṇenaiva vartulaṁ bhāti sūryavat

tadvadātmani dehatvaṁ paśyatyajñānayogataḥ

alātam	n. coal, firebrand,
bhramaṇenaiva	
bhramaṇena	3/s/n through, by, with rotation, turning round, roaming,
eva	indeed, only, alone,
vartulam	2/s mfn, m. n. round, ring, circle,
bhāti	appears, shines, manifests, 1/s/pres/act √*bhā*
sūryavat	like the sun
tadvat	so, similarly
ātmani	7/s/m in the Self
dehatvam	2/s having the nature of the body
paśyati	he sees
ajñāna	n. ignorance, mfn unwise, of ignorance
yogataḥ	3/s by contact of, by means of, by contact with, (*ta* - 2ndary suffix indicating possession or measure),

79. As a fire-brand just through being whirled around appears circular like the sun, so a person in ignorance sees the Self as having the characteristics of the body.

⊡

महत्त्वे सर्ववस्तूनामणुत्वं ह्यतिदूरतः ।

तद्वदात्मनि देहत्वं पश्यत्यज्ञानयोगतः ॥८०॥

mahattve sarvavastūnāmaṇutvaṁ hyatidūrataḥ

tadvadātmani dehatvaṁ paśyatyajñānayogataḥ

mahattve	7/s/n in greatness, in largeness
sarvavastūnāmaṇutvam	*sarva* all
-vastūnām	6/pl/n of things, items, objects,
-aṇutvam	2/s/n atomic nature, minuteness,
hyatidūrataḥ	*hi* ind. for, since, because,
-atidūrataḥ	*atidūra* mfn very distant, very far, n. very far away, great distance, (*ta* - 2ndary suffix indicating possession or measure), having great distance,
tadvat	so, similarly
ātmani	7/s/m in the Self
dehatvam	2/s having the nature of the body
paśyati	he sees
ajñāna	n. ignorance, mfn unwise, of ignorance
yogataḥ	3/s by contact of, by means of, by contact with

80. In large things there may seem to be minuteness when viewed from far away. Similarly a person in ignorance sees the Self as having the nature of the body.

⊡

सूक्ष्मत्वे सर्वभावानां स्थूलत्वं चोपनेत्रतः ।

तद्वदात्मनि देहत्वं पश्यत्यज्ञानयोगतः ॥८१॥

sūkṣmatve sarvabhāvānāṁ sthūlatvaṁ copanetrataḥ

tadvadātmani dehatvaṁ paśyatyajñānayogataḥ

sūkṣmatve	7/s mfn in having the nature of the fine, tiny, atomic, delicate,
sarvabhāvānām	6/pl/ of all objects
sthūlatvam	2/s having the nature of being large, coarse, bulky, thick, massive, stupid, gross, dull,
ca	and
upanetrataḥ	n. lenses, spectacles, (+*ta*) having,
tadvat	so, similarly
ātmani	7/s/m in the Self
dehatvam	2/s having the nature of the body
paśyati	he sees
ajñāna	n. ignorance, mfn unwise, of ignorance
yogataḥ	3/s by contact of, by means of, by contact with,

81. As the smallness of tiny objects may appear large through a lens, similarly a person in ignorance sees the Self as having the nature of the body.

काचभूमौ जलत्वं वा जलभूमौ हि काचता ।

तद्वदात्मनि देहत्वं पश्यत्यज्ञानयोगतः

kācabhūmau jalatvaṁ vā jalabhūmau hi kācatā
tadvadātmani dehatvaṁ paśyatyajñānayogataḥ

kāca	n.m. glass, *bhūmau* 7/s/f land, earth, floor, ground, surface? in/on a surface of glass
jalatvam	2/s having the characteristics of water
vā	or
jalabhūmau	on the surface of water,
hi	ind. for, since, because,
kācatā	having the nature of glass, glassiness,
tadvat	so, similarly
ātmani	7/s/m in the Self
dehatvam	2/s having the nature of the body
paśyati	he sees
ajñāna	n. ignorance, mfn unwise, of ignorance
yogataḥ	3/s by contact of, by means of, by contact with,

82. As a glass surface may look like water or water may appear to be glassy, so similarly a person in ignorance sees the Self as having the characteristics of the body.

यद्वदग्नौ मणित्वं हि मणौ वा वह्निता पुमान् ।

तद्वदात्मनि देहत्वं पश्यत्यज्ञानयोगतः ।।८३।।

yadvadagnau maṇitvaṁ hi maṇau vā vahnitā pumān

tadvadātmani dehatvaṁ paśyatyajñānayogataḥ

yadvat	as, in which way
agnau	7/s/m in fire
maṇitvam	2/s having the nature of a jewel or gem,
hi	as, for, since, because,
maṇau	7/s/m in a jewel or gem
vā	emphasis/filler
vahnitā	*vahni* fire, +*tā* having firiness
pumān	1/s/m *puṁs* a man
tadvat	so, similarly
ātmani	7/s/m in the Self
dehatvam	2/s having the nature of the body
paśyati	he sees
ajñāna	n. ignorance, mfn unwise, of ignorance
yogataḥ	3/s by contact of, by means of, by contact with,

83. As a man sees fieryness in a jewel or sees jewels in a fire, so similarly a person in ignorance sees the Self as having the characteristics of the body.

◘

अभ्रेषु सत्सु धावत्सु सोमो भाति वै ।

तद्वदात्मनि देहत्वं पश्यत्यज्ञानयोगतः॥८३॥

abhreṣu satsu dhāvatsu somo bhāti vai
tadvadātmani dehatvaṁ paśyatyajñānayogataḥ

abhreṣu	7/pl/m in clouds
satsu	7/pl/m in existences, being
dhāvatsu	7/pl/mfn quick, running
somaḥ	1/s/m the moon, nectar, plant,
bhāti	it appears, manifests 1/s/pres/act √*bhā*
vai	emphasis/filler
tadvat	so, similarly
ātmani	7/s/m in the Self
dehatvam	2/s having the nature of the body
paśyati	he sees
ajñāna	n. ignorance, mfn unwise, of ignorance
yogataḥ	3/s by contact of, by means of, by contact with,

84. In quickly moving clouds the moon appears to be moving. Similarly a person in ignorance sees the Self as having the characteristics of the body.

◻

यथैव दिग्विपर्यासो मोहाद्भवति कस्यचित् ।
तद्वदात्मनि देहत्वं पश्यत्यज्ञानयोगतः ॥८५॥

yathaiva digviparyāso mohādbhavati kasyacit
tadvadātmani dehatvaṁ paśyatyajñānayogataḥ

yathaiva	ind. just as
digviparyāsaḥ	*dig (dik)* quarter or region pointed at, direction, cardinal point, *-viparyāsa* m. error, mistake, imagining what is false to be true,
mohāt	5/s/m from, through delusion,
bhavati	it becomes, appears, is, manifests,
kasyacit	of someone or something, of one, someone
tadvat	so, similarly
ātmani	7/s/m in the Self
dehatvam	2/s having the nature of the body
paśyati	he sees
ajñāna	n. ignorance, mfn unwise, of ignorance
yogataḥ	3/s by contact of, by means of, by contact with,

85. Just as someone mistakes directions through delusion so similarly a person in ignorance sees the Self as having the characteristics of the body.

□

यथा शशी जले भाति चञ्चलत्वेन कस्यचित् ।

तद्वदात्मनि देहत्वं पश्यत्यज्ञानयोगतः ॥८६॥

yathā śaśī jale bhāti cañcalatvena kasyacit
tadvadātmani dehatvaṁ paśyatyajñānayogataḥ

yathā	as, like,
śaśī	the moon
jale	7/s in water
bhāti	appears, manifests
cañcalatvena	*cañcala* mfn unsteady, quivering, moving, flickering
kasyacit	of someone or something, of one, someone
tadvat	so, similarly
ātmani	7/s/m in the Self
dehatvam	2/s having the nature of the body
paśyati	he sees
ajñāna	n. ignorance, mfn unwise, of ignorance
yogataḥ	3/s by contact of, by means of, by contact with,

86. Just as the moon reflected in water appears to be in motion, so a person in ignorance sees the Self as having the nature of the body.

एवमात्मन्यविद्यातो देहाध्यासो हि जायते ।

स एवात्मपरिज्ञानाल्लीयते च परात्मनि ।।८७।।

evamātmanyavidyāto dehādhyāso hi jāyate

sa evātmaparijñānāllīyate ca parātmani

evam	thus
ātmani	in the Self
avidyātaḥ	through being ignorant
deha	(of) the body
adhyāsaḥ	1/s case of mistaken identity
hi	for, since, because,
jāyate	1/s/pass/ √*jan* arises, comes into existence, is born,
sa	he, that
eva	ind. indeed, only, alone
ātmaparijñānāllīyate	*ātma* the Self
-parijñānāt	n. through knowledge, serendipity, discrimination, perception,
-līyate	1/s/pass/ √*lī ?* disappears, hides, clings, sticks to,
ca	and
parātmani	7/s/mfn in one who considers the body as the soul, m. Supreme Spirit,

87. Thus through ignorance the body is mistaken for the Self. Through discrimination the delusion vanishes since the Self alone exists.

◘

सर्वमात्मतया ज्ञातं जगत् स्थावरजङ्गमम् ।

अभावात् सर्वभावानां देहस्य चात्मता कुतः ॥८८॥

sarvamātmatayā jñātaṁ jagat sthāvarajaṅgamam

abhāvāt sarvabhāvānāṁ dehasya cātmatā kutaḥ

sarvam	all, everything,
ātmatayā	as if the Self, as if one's true Self,
jñātam	2/s/ mfn known
jagat	the world, the universe
sthāvara	mfn unmoving
jaṅgamam	mfn moving, movable,
abhāvāt	5/s/m *abhāva* non-existence, non-entity, nullity, negation, through negation,
sarvabhāvānāṁ	sarva all, *bhāva* things 6/pl of all things,
dehasya	of the body
ca	and
ātmatā	f. nature, essence, the quality of being the Self
kutaḥ	where

88. When the whole moving and unmoving universe is known as one's own Self through the negation of all things, then how could the body be the Self?

आत्मानं सततं जानन् कालं नय महाद्युते ।

प्रारब्धमखिलं भुञ्जन्नोद्वेगं कर्तुमर्हसि ।।८९।।

ātmānaṁ satataṁ jānan kālaṁ naya mahādyute

prārabdhamakhilaṁ bhuñjannodvegaṁ kartumarhasi

ātmānam 2/s/m the Self

satatam mfn/adv. continual, perpetual, eternal, constantly, continuously

jānan pres. part. knowing, understanding, realizing,

kālam 2/s time

naya m. prudent conduct or behaviour, leading thought, principle,
mfn right, proper

mahādyute mfn of great splendour, very bright, glorious,
voc. O splendid one,

prārabdhamakhilam

prārabdham 'the circumstances one encounters due to good or bad saṁskāra'

akhilam mfn whole, entire, without a gap, complete, n. universe

bhuñjannodvegam

bhuñjan pres.part. bhuj cl7. ? enjoying, experiencing,

-na not, without,

-udvegam 2/s/m fuss, tranquil, anxiety, fear, distress,

kartum inf. √*kṛ* to do, make, perform,

arhasi 2/s/pres/act √*arh* you be worthy of, be able to, be able, deserve,

89. O Splendid One, be worthy of ever knowing the Self, living rightly and tranquilly while experiencing without fuss the karma from the past bearing fruit in the present.

उत्पन्नेऽप्यात्मविज्ञाने प्रारब्धं नैव मुञ्चति ।

इति यच्छ्रूयते शास्त्रे तन्निराक्रियतेऽधुना ॥९०॥

utpanne'pyātmavijñāne prārabdhaṁ naiva muñcati
iti yacchrū yate śāstre tannirākriyate'dhunā

utpanne'pyātmavijñāne *utpanne* 7/s/n in the product, mfn produced, come forth, appeared, risen, output (production),
-api ind. also, too, even, nevertheless,
-ātma (of) the Self
-vijñāne 7/s in knowledge (of the Self)
prārabdham 'the circumstances one encounters due to good or bad *saṁskāra*'
naiva *na eva* not indeed
muñcati grants, discharges, lets loose, frees, sets free, goes, sends forth,
iti end of quote,
yat which, what, who
śrūyate is heard
śāstre 7/s in scripture
tannirākriyate'dhunā *tat* that
-nirākriyate 1/s/pres/pass *nir ā* √*kṛ* P. to separate or drive off, to drive away, repudiate, remove, reject, omi, refuse, oppose,
-adhunā ind. at this time, now,

90. It is heard in scripture that even after Self-knowledge has arisen *prārabdha* is not destroyed. That statement will now be refuted.

तत्त्वज्ञानोदयादूर्ध्वं प्रारब्धं नैव विद्यते ।

देहादीनामसत्त्वात्तु यथा स्वप्नो विबोधतः ॥९१॥

tattvajñānodayādūrdhvaṁ prārabdhaṁ naiva vidyate

dehādīnāmasattvāttu yathā svapno vibodhataḥ

tattvajñānodayādūrddhaṁ *tattva* n. true or real state, truth, reality, in phil. a true principle

-jñānaḥ	m. knowledge, higher or spiritual knowledge,
-udayāt	5/s *udaya* m. emerging, coming forward, consequence,
ūrdhvam	2/s ind. after (with 5th)
prārabdham	'the circumstances one encounters due to good or bad *saṁskāra*'
naiva	na eva not even, not indeed,
vidyate	is known, found 1/s/pres/pass/*vid*

dehādīnāmasattvāttu *deha* the body, of the body

-ādīnām	*ādi* 6/pl beginning with, and the like
-asat	mfn non-existent, unreal, untrue,
-tvāt	*tva* having the nature of, 5/s from
-tu	but
yathā	as, like
svapnaḥ	1/s dream
vibodhataḥ	mfn awakening, awakened,

91. After realization of the knowledge of reality, *prārabdha* is not known because the body and everything to do with it has no existence just as a dream has no reality after waking.

कर्म जन्मान्तरीयं यत् प्रारब्धमिति कीर्तितम् ।

तत्तु जन्मान्तराभावात् पुंसो नैवास्ति कर्हिचित् ॥९२॥

karma janmāntarīyaṁ yat prārabdhamiti kīrtitam

tattu janmāntarābhāvāt puṁso naivāsti karhicit

karma	*karma*
janmāntarīyam	2/s done in a former life,
yat	which, what,
prārabdham	*prārabdha*
iti	end of quote, thus,
kīrtitam	2/s said, mentioned, asserted, celebrated, known,
tattu	*tat* that, *tu* but,
janmāntara	n. another birth or life, a former life, a future life,
abhāvāt	he/it became, 1/s/impf/ √*bhū*
puṁsaḥ	5/6/s of a/the man
naivāsti	*na eva asti* not even is
karhicit	at any time, ever,

92. Karma which is from a previous life is known as *prārabdha* but a future birth does not exist for a (realised) man.

स्वप्नदेहो यथाध्यस्तस्तथैवायं हि देहकः ।

अध्यस्तस्य कुतो जन्म जन्माभावे हि तत् कुतः ।।९३।।

svapnadeho yathādhyastastathaivāyaṁ hi dehakaḥ

adhyastasya kuto janma janmābhāve hi tat kutaḥ

svapna	(in) dream
-dehaḥ	the body
yathā	as, like,
adhyastaḥ	mfn disguised, supposed, placed over, superimposed,
tathā	so
eva	indeed
ayam	this
hi	for, since, because,
dehakaḥ	1/s the body
adhyastasya	6/s of (that) superimposition
kutaḥ	interr. adv. from where, whence,
janma	m.n. birth,
janma-	birth
-abhāve	7/s/m in non-existence,
hi	for, since, because,
tat	that, *(prārabdha)*
kutaḥ	whence

93. Just as in a dream the (illusion of a) body is super-imposed, so indeed this body is also just an (illusory) superimposition (on the Ātman). From where could *prārabdha* be born if birth is non-existent?

उपादानं प्रपञ्चस्य मृद्भाण्डस्येव कथ्यते ।

अज्ञानं चैव वेदान्तैस्तस्मिन्नष्टे क्व विश्वता ।।९४।।

upādānaṁ prapañcasya mṛdbhāṇḍasyeva kathyate
ajñānaṁ caiva vedāntaistasminnaṣṭe kva viśvatā

upādānam	1/2/s/n material cause, application, use, motive,
prapañcasya	6/s of development, appearance, trick, fraud, visible world, manifestation or form of diffuseness,
mṛdbhāṇḍasyeva	*mṛd* of clay, earth,
-bhāṇḍasya	6/s of a vessel, pail, jar,
-iva	ind. as if, like,
kathyate	is regarded as, to be called, be regarded or considered as,
ajñānam	2/s ignorance,
caiva	*ca* and, *eva* indeed
vedāntais	3/pl by/with the *Vedānta* (texts)
tasmin	pron. 7/s in that
naṣṭe	7/s mfn in vain, lost, deprived of, disappeared, destroyed, corrupted, fruitless, perished,
kva	ind. wherever, nowhere, where, in a certain place,
viśvatā	f. abstract noun from *viśvam* all, everything, the universe,

94. The Upaniṣads say the cause of the visible world is ignorance just as the material cause of a jar is clay. If ignorance disappeared then where would be the universe?

यथा रज्जुं परित्यज्य सर्पं गृह्णाति वै भ्रमात् ।

तद्वत् सत्यमविज्ञाय जगत् पश्यति मूढधीः ।।९५।।

yathā rajjuṁ parityajya sarpaṁ gṛhṇāti vai bhramāt

tadvat satyamavijñāya jagat paśyati mūḍhadhīḥ

yathā	as, like,
rajjum	2/s a rope
parityajya	ind. at a distance from,
sarpam	2/s a snake
gṛhṇāti	1/s/pres/act √grah, he takes, lays hold of, perceives (grabbed by the eye),
vai	indeed
bhramāt	5/s *bhrama* m roaming about, unsteadiness, rotation, error, mistake, from error
tadvat	ind. in the same way,
satyamavijñāya	*satyam* truth, reality,
-avijñāya	*vijñāya* mfn recognizable, avijñāya not recognizable, unknown,
jagat	the world
paśyati	he sees 1/s/pres/act √paś
mūḍhadhīḥ	mfn mfn simple, foolish, silly-minded,

95. As a rope when seen from a distance may appear to be a snake so in the same way an ignorant person sees the world while not recognising the reality.

रज्जुरूपे परिज्ञाते सर्पखण्डं न तिष्ठति ।

अधिष्ठने तथा ज्ञाते प्रपञ्चः शून्यतां गतः ॥९६॥

rajjurūpe parijñāte sarpakhaṇḍam na tiṣṭhati

adhiṣṭhane tathā jñāte prapañcaḥ śūnyatāṁ gataḥ

rajjurūpe 7/s when the form of the rope

parijñāte 7/s in ascertained, learned, recognised, thoroughly known,

sarpakhaṇḍam *sarpa* (of) the snake

-*khaṇḍam* 2/s slice, bit, piece, divided, not full, deficient,

na not

tiṣṭhati 1/s/pres/act√*sthā* stays, remains, abides, stands

adhiṣṭhane 7/s/n precedent, residence, standing over, standing or resting upon, base of support, substratum,

tathā so

jñāte *jñāta* mfn 7/s known, learnt, meant, ascertained, perceived,

prapañcaḥ 1/s/m the visible world,

śūnyatā 2/s f. loneliness, non-existence, vacancy, emptiness, illusory nature of phenomena, non-reality,

gataḥ mfn gone,

96. When the form of the rope is recognised then the unreality of the snake does not remain (in mind) so, in the same way, when the substratum is known, then the visible world (having the illusory nature of phenomena) goes.

◻

देहस्यापि प्रपञ्चत्वात् प्रारब्धावस्थितिः कुतः ।

अज्ञानिजनबोधार्थं प्रारब्धं वक्ति वै श्रुतिः ॥९७॥

dehasyāpi prapañcatvāt prārabdhāvasthitiḥ kutaḥ

ajñānijanabodhārthaṁ prārabdhaṁ vakti vai śrutiḥ

dehasya	6/s of the body
api	ind. also
prapañcatvāt	*prapañca* the visible world, *-tva* having the nature of, 5/s from having the nature of the material world, and body
prārabdhāvasthitiḥ	*prārabdha* 'the circumstances one encounters due to good or bad *saṁskāra*'
-avasthitiḥ	f. residence, abiding, stability, following, practising,
kutaḥ	ind. from where, why,
ajñānijanabodhārtham	*ajñāni* ignorant 1/pl. how
-jana	people, persons,
-bodhārtham	cause of awakening for the awakening of the ignorant,
prārabdham	2/s as above
vakti	1/s/pres/act *vac* speaks, says,
vai	indeed, only
śrutiḥ	revealed scripture

97. The body is naturally in the material world so how could it follow the circumstances one encounters due to good or bad saṁskāra? *Prārabdha* is only spoken of in the revealed scriptures for the awakening of the ignorant.

◻

क्षीयन्ते चास्य कर्माणि तस्मिन् दृष्टे परावरे ।

बहुत्वं तन्निषेधार्थं श्रुत्या गीतं च यत् स्फुटम् ॥९८॥

kṣīyante cāsya karmāṇi tasmin dṛṣṭe parāvare

bahutvaṁ tanniṣedhārthaṁ śrutyā gītaṁ ca yat sphuṭam

kṣīyante 1/pl/pres/pass √*4. kṣi* to be diminished, decrease, wane, waste away, perish, are wasted away, perish, are diminished,

ca asya and, of that

karmāṇi 1/2/pl/n actions

tasmin *pron.* in that

dṛṣṭe *dṛṣṭa* ppp. 7/s in perceived, imagined, acknowledged, beheld, understood, realised,

parāvare 7/s, mfn in earlier and later, distant and near, highest and lowest, all-including, n. cause and effect, universe,

bahutvam 2nd n. plurality, majority, multitude, abundance,

tanniṣedhārtham *tat* that, of that

-niṣedha m. prohibition, denial, negation,

-artham 2/s cause, reason for, for the negation of that

śrutyā 3/s *śruti* by the *śruti* (revealed texts)

gītam 2/s/ ppp. √*gṝ* to call, call out to, invoke, announce, proclaim, praise, announced, proclaimed, invoked, called out to,

ca and, *tat* who, which,

sphuṭam 2/s/ mfn open, opened, expanded, blossomed, manifest, evident, clear, ind. clearly,

98. (The effects of) past actions disappear in that all-including realisation (of the Self). The word *bahutvam* (plurality) is clearly used by the revealed texts for the negation of *prārabdha*.

⊡

उच्यतेऽज्ञैर्बलाच्चैतत्तदानर्थद्वयागमः ।
वेदान्तमतहानं च यतो ज्ञानमिति श्रुतिः ॥९९॥

ucyate'jñairbalāccaitattadānarthadvayāgamaḥ
vedāntamatahānaṁ ca yato jñānamiti śrutiḥ

ucyate'jñairbalāccaitattadānarthadvayāgamaḥ *ucyate* 1/s/pres/pass √*vac* to speak, say, tell, be regarded as, be called or accounted for,
-*ajñaiḥ* 3/pl/m through ignorance,
-*balāt* 5/s/n from power, stamina, force,
-*ca* and
-*etat* this, pron. 1/s/n, *tadā* ind. then
anarthadvayāgamaḥ *anartha* mfn having no meaning, useless, worthless
-*dvaya* two
-*āgamaḥ* 1/s/m principle, theory, approach, collection of doctrines, two worthless arguments,
vedāntamatahānaṁ *vedānta* the *Upaniṣads*
-*mata* n. advice, religion, vote, mfn regarded as, honoured, thought fit,
-*hānam* 2/s/n giving up, relinquishing, abandoning, relinquishing the advice of the *Upaniṣads*
ca and
yataḥ mfn because, governed, controlled, ind. since, from where
jñānam 2/s/m knowledge, higher knowledge,
iti thus, end of quote,
śrutiḥ *śruti* revealed truth

99. (If this doctrine) is held to through the power of ignorance then (holding to these) two absurdities (which imply duality) would effectively mean forsaking the instruction of *Vedānta*, the true knowledge. Thus one should hold to the revealed truth.

One should hold to *śruti* remembering that the whole thrust of *Vedānta* is towards Advaita (non-duality) and therefore any non-duality would be inconsistent. The theory that prārabdha continues after realisation implies bondage after freedom which would be a duality because there would always be a second. The second situation is that accepting the continuing *prārabdha* argument invalidates the tenets of Vedānta which are the basis of this philosophical system.

त्रिपञ्चाङ्गान्यथो वक्ष्ये पूर्वोक्तस्य हि लब्धये ।

तैश्च सर्वैः सदा कार्यं निदिध्यासनमेव तु ॥१००॥

tripañcāṅgānyatho vakṣye pūrvoktasya hi labdhaye

taiśca sarvaiḥ sadā kāryaṁ nididhyāsanameva tu

tripañcāṅgānyatho	*tri*	3
pañca	5	3x5 = 15
āṅgāni	1/2/pl/n members or divisions, parts, steps,	
athaḥ	now,	
vakṣye	I shall explain	
pūrvoktasya	*pūrva* mfn previous, former	
uktasya	6/s/mfn *ukta* mfn spoken, said, 6/s of that	
	having spoken of that previously mentioned	
hi	for, since, emphasis,	
labdhaye	4/s gained for, for attainment,	
taiḥ	pron. 3/pl by those/these	
ca	and	
sarvaiḥ	3/pl pron. by all	
sadā	ind. always, ever, perpetually,	
kāryam	2/s to be done or practised,	
nididhyāsanam	2/s/n profound and repeated meditation.	
eva	ind. indeed, only, alone, *tu* but, and	

100. Now I shall explain the 15 steps (through which) the knowledge previously spoken of for enlightenment may be gained by all through the practise of continuous profound meditation.

⊡

नित्याभ्यासादृते प्राप्ति र्न भवेत् सच्चिदात्मनः ।

तस्माद् ब्रह्म निदिध्यासेज्जिज्ञासुः श्रेयसे चिरम् ॥१०१॥

nityābhyāsādṛte prāpti rna bhavet saccidātmanaḥ

tasmād brahma nididhyāsejjijñāsuḥ śreyase ciram

nityābhyāsādṛte *nitya* mfn perpetual, everlasting, constant, necessary,

-abhyāsāt *5/s/*m habit, drill, practice, repetition,

-ṛte ind. unless, except, without, without constant repetition, practice

prāptiḥ *prāpti* m. obtaining, gain, f. act of acquisition, achievement,

na not

bhavet he/it should/may/could become, arise, 1/s/act/opt/ √*bhū*

saccidātmanaḥ *sat* pres.part. existing, being present, existence,

-cit mfn conscious, perceive, think, thought, intellect, knowledge,

-ātmanaḥ 5/6/s/m of the Self

tasmāt pron. from that, therefore

brahma the *Brahman*

nididhyāsejjijñāsuḥ *nididhyāset* he should meditate profoundly and repeatedly, 1/s/opt/act

jijñāsu mfn 1/s from desid. √*jñā* the one desiring to learn or know,

śreyase 4/s/n *śreyasa* for welfare, bliss, happiness,

ciram ind. for a long time,

101. Without constant attentive practice the knowledge of the present existence of the Self may not arise from that Brahman.

Therefore (the aspirant) should meditate profoundly and repeatedly over a long period of time for the welfare, bliss and happiness (of all).

यमो हि नियमस्त्यागो मौनं देशश्च कालता ।

आसनं मूलबन्धश्च देहसाम्यं च दृक्स्थितिः ॥१०२॥

yamo hi niyamastyāgo maunaṁ deśaśca kālatā

āsanaṁ mūlabandhaśca dehasāmyaṁ ca dṛksthitiḥ

yamaḥ	1/s/m self-control, forbearance,
hi	so, for, since, because,
niyamaḥ	1/s/m restraint of the mind,
tyāgaḥ	1/s/m renunciation,
maunam	1/s/n silence, taciturnity,
deśaḥ	1/s/m place, country, spot,
ca	and
kālatā	1/s/f timeliness,
āsanam	1/s/n abiding, sitting, posture, particular posture of devotee,
mūlabandhaḥ	mfn deep-rooted
ca	and
dehasāmyam	1/s/n equilibrium, poise, balance of the body
ca	and
dṛksthitiḥ	1/s steadiness of gaze

The translation of verses 102 and 103 has been combined because this is the way that they would naturally flow. Each item on the list is then expanded on.

प्राणसंयमनं चैव प्रत्याहारश्च धारणा ।

आत्मध्यानं समाधिश्च प्रोक्तान्यङ्गानि वै क्रमात् ॥१०३॥

prāṇasaṁyamanaṁ caiva pratyāhāraśca dhāraṇā

ātmadhyānaṁ samādhiśca proktānyaṅgāni vai kramāt

prāṇasaṁyamanam	1/s/n suppression or suspension of the breath
ca	and
eva	indeed, only, alone,
pratyāhāraḥ	1/s/m withdrawal (e.g. of senses from external objects)
ca	and
dhāraṇā	1/s/f steadfastness, concentration,
ātmadhyānam	meditation on the Self
samādhiḥ	profound absorption
ca	and
proktāni	1/pl/n declared, spoken, taught, proclaimed,
aṅgāni	1/pl/n the steps,
vai	emphasis on previous word,
kramāt	5/s/m *krama,* from, through succession, step by step,

102/103. The steps listed in order are -
self-control, restraint of the mind, renunciation, silence or speaking only when necessary, being in the right place or a suitable place, timeliness - meditating at the right time of day and for the prescribed length of time, correct posture, *mūlabandhaḥ* - a particular posture to be used with particular yogic disciplines, equilibrium of the body, steadiness of gaze (eyes still), suppression or suspension of the breath (like *mūlabandhaḥ* - only to be attempted with qualified instruction and according to the path being followed), withdrawal (e.g. of senses from external objects), steadfastness of concentration, meditation on the Self, and profound absorption.

सर्वं ब्रह्मेति विज्ञानादिन्द्रियग्रामसंयमः ।

यमोऽयमिति संप्रोक्तोऽभ्यसनीयो मुहुर्मुहुः ॥१०४॥

sarvaṁ brahmeti vijñānādindriyagrāmasaṁyamaḥ

yamo'yamiti saṁprokto'bhyasanīyo muhurmuhuḥ

sarvam all

brahma *Brahman*

iti end of quote

vijñānādindriyagrāmasaṁyamaḥ *vijñānāt* n. the act of distinguishing or discerning, understanding, comprehending, recognizing, intelligence, knowledge,

indriyagrāma m. the assemblage of the organs, the senses or organs of sense collectively,

saṁyamaḥ 1/s/m holding together, restraint, control, esp. control of the senses, concentration of mind; comprising the performance of *dhāraṇā, dhyāna, and samādhi,*

yamaḥ a rein, curb, bridle, the act of checking or curbing, restraint,

ayam pron. 1/s this, *iti* end of quote, thus,

saṁprokto'bhyasanīyo

saṁproktaḥ ind. well-spoken, announced, declared, called,

abhyasanīyaḥ mfn to be practised, to be studied or repeated,

muhurmuhuḥ 1/s/m again and again, repeatedly,

104. Through acts of discrimination such as contemplation of "All this is Brahman" in steadfast concentration, the organs of sense are restrained. This practice called *Yama* is to be practised again and again.

◘

सजातीयप्रवाहश्च विजातीयतिरस्कृतिः ।

नियमो हि परानन्दो नियमात् क्रियते बुधैः ॥१०५॥

sajātīyapravāhaśca vijātīyatiraskṛtiḥ

niyamo hi parānando niyamāt kriyate budhaiḥ

sajātīyapravāhaśca	*sajātīya* mfn resembling, similar, of the same kind, like,
pravāhaḥ	1/s/m flow, current, continuous train of thought, continuous flow of the same train of thought,
ca	and
vijātīyatiraskṛtiḥ	*vijātīya* mfn dissimilar, different origin,
tiras	ind. through, across, beyond, over, without, against, apart, secretly,
kṛtiḥ	f. the act of doing, making, performing, action, activity, without other (thoughts) or (thoughts) from elsewhere,
niyamaḥ	1/s/m checking, holding back, restraining, limitation, restriction to, determination, necessity, obligation, vow,
hi	emphasis, for, since, because,
parānandaḥ	1/s/m supreme bliss,
niyamāt	5/s/m *niyama* from/ through preventing, restraining, determination, holding back
kriyate	1/s/pres/pass √*kṛ* is done, made, performed, practised,
budhaiḥ	3/pl/m *budha* by the wise

105. Continuous flow of the same train of thought without thoughts from anywhere else is called *niyama*. Supreme bliss through *niyama* is practised by the wise.

Note: The train of thought should be about identity with Brahman.

त्यागः प्रपञ्चरूपस्य चिदात्मत्वावलोकनात् ।

त्यागो हि महतां पूज्यः सद्यो मोक्षमयो यतः ।।१०६।।

tyāgaḥ prapañcarūpasya cidātmatvāvalokanāt

tyāgo hi mahatāṁ pūjyaḥ sadyo mokṣamayo yataḥ

tyāgaḥ	1/s/m leaving, abandoning, forsaking, abandonment,
prapañcarūpasya	*prapañca* m. expansion, development, manifestation, the visible world, the phenomenal universe,
rūpasya	6/s/n of the form, shape, figure, nature
cidātmatvāvalokanāt	*cidātmatva* having the nature of the conscious Self,
avalokanāt	5/s/n from/through seeing, observing, realizing, realising it as having the nature of the conscious Self,
tyāgaḥ	1/s/m abandoning, renunciation,
hi	ind. for, since, because, emphasis,
mahatām	2/s/f greatness, mightiness,
pūjyaḥ	m. an honourable man, mfn to be revered or worshipped, venerable, honourable,
sadyaḥ	ind. in the very moment, -at once, immediately, just, recently, on the same day, daily, every day,
mokṣamayaḥ	consisting of liberation, having the nature of, filled with,
yataḥ	mfn because,

106. The abandonment of the phenomenal nature of the universe through realising it as having the nature of the conscious Self is true renunciation. Its greatness is revered for it has the effect of instant liberation.

⊡

यस्माद्वाचो निवर्तन्ते अप्राप्य मनसा सह ।

यन्मौनं योगिभिर्गम्यं तद्भवेत् सर्वदा बुधः ॥१०७॥

yasmādvāco nivartante aprāpya manasā saha

yanmaunaṁ yogibhirgamyaṁ tadbhvet sarvadā budhaḥ

yasmāt	from which
vācāḥ	1/pl/f words
nivartante	1/pl/pres/mid √*vṛt* they come back, they turn back,
aprāpya	ind. having failed to reach or attain,
manasā	ind. in thought or imagination, in the mind, willingly,
saha	ind. with, together with,
yat	ind. which
maunam	1/2/s/n silence, office of a sage, taciturnity,
yogibhiḥ	3/pl/m by the yogis,
gamyam	mfn approachable, suitable, attainable, perceptible,
tad	pron. that
bhavet	1/s/opt/ √*bhū* should be, could be
sarvadā	at all times,
budhaḥ	1/s/m wise, god, learned man,

107. That silence (of the mind) from which words together with the mind turn back having failed to attain is attainable by the yogis. The wise should at all times be That (silence).

⊡

वाचो यस्मान्निवर्तन्ते तद्वक्तुं केन शक्यते ।

प्रपञ्चो यदि वक्तव्यः सोऽपि शब्दविवर्जितः ॥१०८॥

vāco yasmānnivartante tadvaktuṁ kena śakyate

prapañco yadi vaktavyaḥ so'pi śabdavivarjitaḥ

vācaḥ	1/pl/f words
yasmāt	from which
nivartante	1/pl/pres/mid √*vṛt* they come back, they turn back,
tat	pron. that
vaktum	infin. √*vac* to speak, say, describe, utter, tell,
kena	3/s/pron. by that, with that, by whom,
śakyate	1/s/pres/pass is able or competent,
prapañcaḥ	1/s/m expansion, development, manifestation, the visible world, the phenomenal universe,
yadi	ind. if, in case,
vaktavyaḥ	mfn fit to be said, n. statement, to be named or called, to be spoken of or said about,
so'pi	*saḥ* he, that,
api	ind. also, even
śabdavivarjitaḥ	*śabda-* words,
-vivarjitaḥ	mfn excepting, free from, excluding, without words,

108. Who is competent to describe that from which words turn back ? Even if the physical world is to be spoken of it is indescribable. Note:It is in truth neither existent nor non-existent due to the illusory nature of *māyā* .

◻

इति वा तद्भवेन्मौनं सतां सहजसंज्ञितम् ।

गिरा मौनं तु बालानां प्रयुक्तं ब्रह्मवादिभिः ॥१०९॥

iti vā tadbhavenmaunaṁ satāṁ sahajasaṁjñitam

girā maunaṁ tu bālānāṁ prayuktaṁ brahmavādibhiḥ

iti	end of quote, thus
vā	ind. or
tadbhavenmaunam	*tat* that
-bhavet	should be, 1/s/opt √*bhū*
-maunam	1/2/s/n silence, office of a sage, taciturnity, silent
satām	6/pl of the devotees, of the truthful, of the sages,
sahajasaṁjñitam	*sahaja* mfn inborn, original, born or produced together,
-saṁjñitam	mfn called, termed, named,
girā	3/s *gira* voice, speech,
maunam	n. silence, position of a muni, taciturnity,
tu	but
bālānām	6/pl *bāla* of children, new or a novice
prayuktam	2/s/mfn appropriate, urged, practised, directed, uttered, prepared, suitable, pronounced,
brahmavādibhiḥ	3/pl/mfn *brahmavādin* one who asserts that all things are to be identified with *Brahman, a Vedāntin,*

109. Or that (internal) silence of the sages could be called original silence (from which everything originates). Also taciturnity or silence (of the lips) is recommended for novices by those who assert that all things are to be identified with Brahman.

⊡

आदावन्ते च मध्ये च जनो यस्मिन्न विद्यते ।

येनेदं सततं व्याप्तं स देशो विजनः स्मृतः ॥११०॥

ādāvante ca madhye ca jano yasminna vidyate

yenedaṁ satataṁ vyāptaṁ sa deśo vijanaḥ smṛtaḥ

ādāvante *ādau* 7/s *ādi* in the beginning,

-ante 7/s *anta* in the end, *ca* and

madhye 7/s *madhya* in the middle, *ca* and

janaḥ 1/s/m person, people, man, common person, the world,

yasmin pron. 7/s in which

na not

vidyate 1/s/pres/pass √*vid* exists, is, there exists,

yena pron. 3/s by which

idam pron. 1/s this

satatam 2/s/mfn perpetual, eternal, constant, continuous, ever

vyāptam 2/s mfn taken possession of, occupied, covered or filled with, fixed, celebrated, rich, full, pervaded

saḥ pron. 1/s that

deśaḥ 1/s/m place, spot, point, (the *Yoga Sūtra* defines *deśa* as a peaceful, calm place for meditation).

vijanaḥ 1/s/mfn free from people, solitary place, deserted,

smṛtaḥ 1/s/mfn enjoined by traditional law, called to mind, remembered, recollected, thought of, prescribed,

110. A place for meditation is prescribed as one in which - the world does not exist in the beginning and in the end and in the middle. A solitary place ever full (of Brahman).

कलनात् सर्वभूतानां ब्रह्मादीनां निमेषतः ।

कालशब्देन निर्दिष्टो ह्यखण्डानन्दकोऽद्वयः ॥१११॥

kalanāt sarvabhūtānāṁ brahmādīnāṁ nimeṣataḥ
kālaśabdena nirdiṣṭo hyakhaṇḍānandako'dvayaḥ

kalanāt	5/s because of causing, effecting, making,
sarvabhūtānāṁ	6/pl of all beings,
brahmādīnāṁ	6/pl of beginning with *Brahmā*
nimeṣataḥ	1/s/f 'twinkler', lightning, the twinkling of an eye
kālaśabdena	3/s by the word time,
nirdiṣṭaḥ	mfn pointed out, shown, indicated, announced, told, ordered, meant or determined for, learned, wise,
hyakhaṇḍānandako'dvayaḥ	*hi* for, since, because, emphasis,
-akhaṇḍa-	mfn whole, entire, undivided, unbroken,
-ānandakaḥ	mfn gladdening, rejoicing, bliss,
advayaḥ	1/s/m assertion of non-duality,

111. The non-dual undivided bliss (Brahman) is known by the word "*kāla*" (time) because in a lightning-flash all beings are created starting from Brahmā.

The Yoga Sūtra defines *kāla* as the proper time to practice *Yoga.*
'Time is the relation between the real Absolute (Brahman) and the non-real appearance name and form (*māyā*) . Thus time is phenomenal.' (Grimes)

सुखेनैव भवेद्यस्मिन्नजस्रं ब्रह्मचिन्तनम् ।

आसनं तद्विजानीयान्नेतरत् सुखनाशनम् ॥११२॥

sukhenaiva bhavedyasminnajasraṁ brahmacintanam

āsanaṁ tadvijānīyānnetarat sukhanāśanam

sukhena	3/s by/with happiness, easily,
-eva	ind. indeed, alone, only,
bhavedyasminnajasraṁ	*bhavet* it should be/become
-yasmin	in which, where,
-ajasram	2/s *ajasra* perpetually, not ceasing,
brahmacintananam	*brahma Brahman*
-cintanam	2/s thinking, thinking of (mental reflection), meditating on Brahman
āsanam	posture
tat	that
-vijānīyāt	he should know, understand,
na	not
itarat(d)	whereas, whilst, any other means,
sukhanāśanam	*sukha* n. happiness, ease,
-nāśanam	2/s/n destruction, loss,

112. One should understand correct posture is that in which meditation on Brahman is unceasing and easy and not any other posture which causes loss of one's ease.

⊡

सिद्धं यत् सर्वभूतादि विश्वाधिष्टानमव्ययम् ।

यस्मिन् सिद्धाः समादिष्टास्तद्वै सिद्धासनं विदुः ॥११३॥

siddhaṁ yat sarvabhūtādi viśvādhiṣṭānamavyayam

yasmin siddhāḥ samādiṣṭāstadvai siddhāsanaṁ viduḥ

siddham 2/s/mfn ready, accomplished, perfected, established,

yat which

sarvabhūtādi all beings from the beginning, origin of all beings or things,

viśvādhiṣṭānamavyayam *viśva-* all

-adhiṣṭānam 2/s/n. steadfast resolution, standing or resting upon,

-avyayam mfn imperishable, not liable to change,

yasmin in which

siddhāḥ 1/pl/m *Siddhās* (the perfected ones)

samādiṣṭāstadvai *samādiṣṭās* mfn absorbed in meditation,

-tat that

-vai emphasis and affirmation,

siddhāsanam 2/s perfect posture (name of a particular posture),

viduḥ 3/pl/perf/act √*vid* they knew, they know or understand,

113. That which is established as the origin of all beings, not subject to change and on which everything rests, and in which the perfected ones are completely absorbed, that they know as *Siddhāsana* the posture of Brahman.

□

यन्मूलं सर्वभूतानां यन्मूलं चित्तबन्दनम् ।
मूलबन्धः सदा सेव्यो योग्योऽसौ राजयोगिनाम् ।।११४।।

yanmūlaṁ sarvabhūtānāṁ yanmūlaṁ cittabandanam
mūlabandhaḥ sadā sevyo yogyo'sau rājayoginām

yat	which
mūlam	2/s mfn original, m. origin, root, source, base,
sarvabhūtānām	6/pl of all beings/things,
yat	which
mūlam	2/s root,
cittabandhanam	2/s binding or restraining of the mind
mūlabandhaḥ	restraining of the root, restraining root,
sadā	ind. at all times, always, ever,
sevyaḥ	1/s/mfn or m. to be studied, honoured or followed, or approached,
yogyaḥ	mfn proper, fit, suitable, fit, useful,
asau	pron. that, a certain,
rājayoginām	6/pl of the rājayogins, suitable for those who practice *Rāja Yoga*

114. That (Brahman) which is the root of all beings and all things, that which gives measure to the mind, is called *Mūlabandha* (the restraining root). There is also a posture for meditation (difficult if not practised from an early age) called by the same name. It is said that it should be followed because it is suitable for those who follow Rāja Yoga (the Royal Way), (a 15th century name for practices based on the Yoga Sutras of Patanjali).

⊡

अङ्गानां समतां विद्यात् समे ब्रह्मणि लीनताम् ।
नो चेन्नैव समानत्वमृजुत्वं शुष्कवृक्षवत् ॥११५॥

aṅgānām samatāṁ vidyāt same brahmaṇi līnatām
no cennaiva samānatvamṛjutvaṁ śuṣkavṛkṣavat

aṅgānām	6/pl of steps, limbs,
samatām	2/s/f equality, equity, equanimity,
vidyāt	he should know 1/s/opt √vid Cl 2
same	7/s in the same, equal,
brahmaṇi	7/s in Brahman
līnatām	2/s/f complete retirement or seclusion, concealment in, merged in, dissolved, absorbed in
na	not
u	a particle implying assent, calling, command, a particle implying restriction and antithesis, with na - slight modification of sense
cennaiva	*cet* ind. if , *na cet* otherwise,
na	not
eva	indeed, only,
samānatvam	2/s/mfn *samāna* mfn equal, same, similar, alike, +*tva* having the nature of
ṛjutvam	2/s/ mfn or m.n. *ṛju* mfn frank, straight, plain, sincere, correctly, in a straight line, +*tva* having the nature of,
śuṣkavṛkṣavat	*śuṣka* mfn dry, withered, dried up,
vṛkṣa	tree
vat	suffix, like, as, like a withered up tree,

115. With his limbs balanced, he should know complete absorption in the constant Brahman and nothing else. If he has only a straight posture then he is like a dried-up tree.

दृष्टिं ज्ञानमयीं कृत्वा पश्येद्ब्रह्ममयं जगत् ।
सा दृष्टिः परमोदारा न नासाग्रावलोकिनी ।।११६।।

dṛṣṭiṁ jñānamayīṁ kṛtvā paśyedbrahmamayaṁ jagat
sā dṛṣṭiḥ paramodārā na nāsāgrāvalokinī

dṛṣṭim	2/s/f vision, sight, wisdom, intelligence, consideration,
jñānamayīm	2/s/mfn consisting of knowledge, full of knowledge,
kṛtvā	ind. having done, made, performed,
paśyedbrahmamayam	*paśyet* he should see, 1/s/opt √*paś*
brahmamayam	2/s mfn consisting of or identified with *Brahman*, belonging to or fit for *Brahman*
jagat	mfn the world,
sā	that
dṛṣṭiḥ	1/s/f vision, sight, wisdom, intelligence, wisdom,
paramodārā	*parama* supreme
-udārā	mfn 1/s/f generous, lenient, liberal, magnanimous,
na	not,
nāsāgrāvalokinī	*nāsāgra* the tip of the nose
avalokin	mfn looking, looking at, beholding
	-*(ī)* 1/s/f looking at the tip of the nose,

116. Having rendered the ordinary view into one full of knowledge he should see the world as Brahman. This is the magnanimous view and not that which beholds the tip of the nose.

द्रष्टृदर्शनदृश्यानां विरामो यत्र वा भवेत् ।

दृष्टिस्तत्रैव कर्तव्या न नासाग्रावलोकिनी ॥११७॥

draṣṭṛdarśanadṛśyānāṁ virāmo yatra vā bhavet

dṛṣṭistatraiva kartavyā na nāsāgrāvalokinī

draṣṭṛdarśanadṛśyānāṁ	
draṣṭṛ-	the seer, the witness
-darśana-	the seeing,
-dṛśyānām	6/pl of the seen
	of the seer, the seeing and the seen
virāmaḥ	m. stop, end, cessation,
yatra	ind. where
vā	ind. or
bhavet	it should be or become 1/s/opt.
dṛṣṭistatraiva	*dṛṣṭiḥ*1/s/f vision, sight, wisdom, intelligence, consideration, wisdom,
tatra	there
eva	indeed, only, alone
kartavyā	f. to be done
na	not
nāsāgrāvalokinī	looking at the tip of the nose, (see previous verse)

117. Where there becomes no distinction between the seer, the seeing and the seen; there alone should there be vision and not looking at the tip of the nose.

चित्तादिसर्वंभावेषु ब्रह्मत्वेनैव भावनात् ।

निरोधः सर्ववृत्तिनां प्राणायामः स उच्यते ॥११८॥

cittādisarvaṁbhāveṣu brahmatvenaiva bhāvanāt

nirodhaḥ sarvavṛttināṁ prāṇāyāmaḥ sa ucyate

cittādisarvaṁbhāveṣu *citta-* n. the heart, mind, intention, aim, wish, attending, observing, thinking,

-ādi- m. beginning, commencement, ind. in the beginning, at first,

-sarvam all

-bhāveṣu 7/pl/m in *bhāva* becoming, being, existing, occurring, appearance, state, thinking, considering, regarding, imagining, in considering everything in the heart and mind

brahmatvenaiva *brahmatvena* 3/s by/through having the nature of *Brahman*

-eva indeed, alone, only

bhāvanāt 5/s from *bhāvanā* mfn causing to be, effecting, producing, manifesting, f. reflection, contemplation, imagining,

nirodhaḥ m. confinement, imprisonment, siege, restraint, check, control,

sarvavṛttināṁ *sarva* all

-vṛttināṁ 6/pl *vṛtti* of f. mode of life or action, course of action, behaviour, common practice, being existing, working, activity,

prāṇāyāmaḥ m. 3 breathing exercises as a part of reflective exercises.

sa that

ucyate 1/s/pres/pass $\sqrt{}$*vac* is called or named,

118. When everything in the heart and mind is considered to be Brahman alone then mental activities are restrained. This practice is called *Prāṇāyāma* (and is described in the next 2 verses).

◻

निषेधनं प्रपञ्चस्य रेचकाख्यः समीरणः ।

ब्रह्मैवास्मीति या पूरको वायुरीरितः ।।११८।।

niṣedhanaṁ prapañcasya recakākhyaḥ samīraṇaḥ
brahmaivāsmīti yā pūrako vāyurīritaḥ

niṣedhanam	2/s/n suppression, control, prevention, prohibition, holding back,
prapañcasya	6/s/ of the natural world,
recakākhyaḥ	*recaka* -mfn emitting the breath, emptying the lungs, breathing out, expelling the breath out of one of the nostrils,
-akhya	named, called, called *recaka*
samīraṇaḥ	mfn setting in motion, causing activity, stimulating,
brahmaivāsmīti	*brahma Brahman*
-eva	indeed
-asmi	I am
-iti	end of quote
yā	which
pūrakaḥ	mfn fulfilling, completing, satisfying, filling, m. act of closing the right nostril with the forefinger and then drawing up air through the left and then closing the left nostril and drawing up air from the right; effusion, stream,
vāyurīritaḥ	*vāyu* m. air, vital air, breath,
īrita	mfn said, uttered, set in motion,

ततस्तद्वृत्तिनैश्चल्यं कुंभकः प्राणसंयमः ।

अयं चापि प्रबुद्धानामज्ञानां घ्राणपीडनम् ।।१२०।।

tatastadvṛttinaiścalyaṁ kuṁbhakaḥ prāṇasaṁyamaḥ
ayaṁ cāpi prabuddhānāmajñānāṁ ghrāṇapīḍanam

tatastadvṛttinaiścalyaṁ *tataḥ* mfn therefore, from that time, due to that,
-tat- that, of that
-vṛtti- activity (of the mind)
naiścalyam 2/s n, immovableness, fixedness,steadiness of that activity of the mind, of thought,
kuṁbhakaḥ m. measure, pot, stopping the breath by shutting the mouth and closing the nostrils with the fingers of the right hand,
prāṇasaṁyamaḥ m. suppression or suspension of the breath,
ayam this
cāpi *ca api* and also
prabuddhānāmajñānāṁ
prabuddhānām 6/pl/mfn of the - mfn awakened, awake, roused, come forth, appeared, known,
ajñānāṁ 6/pl of the ignorant
ghrāṇapīḍanam
ghrāṇa n. smell, nose,
pīḍanam 2/s/n act of pressing or squeezing, squeezing of the nose

119-120. Suppression of the physical world is called *recaka* (breathing out). The idea "I am indeed Brahman" is stimulated by *pūraka* (a breathing in technique). When that idea becomes steady through restricting the breath this is called *kuṁbhaka.* This is the *prāṇāyāma* of the awakened but for the ignorant it is just squeezing the nose.

⧈

विषयेष्वात्मतां दृष्ट्वा मनसश्चितिमज्जनम् ।
प्रत्याहारः स विज्ञेयोऽभ्यसनीयो मुमुक्षुभिः ॥१२१॥

viṣayeṣvātmatāṁ dṛṣṭvā manasaścitimajjanam
pratyāhāraḥ sa vijñeyo'bhyasanīyo mumukṣubhiḥ

viṣayeṣvātmatāṁ	*viṣayeṣu*7/pl in case, theme, content, topic, object, detail,
-ātmatām	2/s essence, the quality or nature of being the self,
dṛṣṭvā	ind. having seen, having realized
manasaścitimajjanam	*manasaḥ* m. the mind
-citi-	7/s *cit,* in consciousness
-majjanam	2/s *majjana* n immersion, sinking, diving
pratyāhāraḥ	1/s *pratyāhāra* m. withdrawing, retreat, withdrawal,
sa	pron. 1/s he, that
vijñeyo'bhyasanīyo	*vijñeya* mfn to be understood or learned or heard, to be perceived or known, knowable, cognizable,
-abhyasanīyaḥ	1/s to be practised, studied, repeated,
mumukṣubhiḥ	3/pl by, with, through eager to be free, desirous of freedom, striving after emancipation,

121. Having recognized the Self in all things he should learn *pratyāhāra* (withdrawal of the mind, absorption into consciousness) for this is to be practised repeatedly by those who strive for freedom.

⊡

यत्र यत्र मनो याति ब्रह्मणस्तत्र दर्शनात् ।

मनसो धारणं चैव धारणा सा परा मता ।।१२२।।

yatra yatra mano yāti brahmaṇastatra darśanāt

manaso dhāraṇaṁ caiva dhāraṇā sā parā matā

yatra yatra	ind. wherever, in that state of affairs where
manas	1/s mind
yāti	it goes, 1/s/pres/ √*yā*
brahmaṇastatra	*brahmaṇaḥ* 5/6/ s of *Brahman*
tatra	ind. there
darśanāt	5/s/ *darśana* mfn seeing, looking, realizing,
manasaḥ	5/6/ s *manas* of /from the mind,
dhāraṇam	1/s/n immovable concentration of the mind upon, act of holding, also mfn or *dhāraṇā*
caiva *ca eva*	and, indeed, only, alone,
dhāraṇā	1/s/f fixing, holding, maintaining, holding, bearing', single-mindedness, to keep in remembrance, (Grimes)
sā	pron. that
parā	supreme
matā	mfn regarded or considered as, known as,

122. Wherever the mind goes see Brahman there.
The act of concentrating the mind on this alone is regarded as the supreme *dhāraṇā* .

ब्रह्मैवास्मीति सद्वृत्त्या निरालम्बतया स्थितिः ।

ध्यानशब्देन विख्याता परमानन्ददायिनी ।।१२३।।

brahmaivāsmīti sadvṛttyā nirālambatayā sthitiḥ

dhyānaśabdena vikhyātā paramānandadāyinī

brahmaivāsmīti	*brahma* *Brahman*
eva	ind. indeed, alone, only,
asmi	I am
iti	end of quote
sadvṛttyā	*sadvṛttyā 3/s/f sadvṛtti* through good conduct, through having good habits, having good character,
nirālambatayā	*nirālambatayā 3/s/ nirālamba* mfn self--supported, independent, friendless, alone,
sthitiḥ	1/s/f standing upright or firmly, not falling, standing, staying, remaining or being in any state or condition,
dhyānaśabdena	*dhyāna* meditation
śabdena	3/s by/with the word, sound,
vikhyātā	1/s/f mfn generally known, known as, called,
paramānandadāyinī	*paramānanda* supreme bliss,
-dāyinī	mfn *dāyin* granting, producing, causing, effecting, granting

123. (Knowing) "I am indeed Brahman" and remaining in this awareness through pure conduct, depending on nothing internal or external is called *dhyāna* (meditation) and enables the supreme bliss to be availed.

निर्विकारतया वृत्त्या ब्रह्माकारतया पुनः
वृत्तिविस्मरणं सम्यक् समाधिर्ज्ञानसंज्ञकः ॥१२४॥

nirvikāratayā vṛttyā brahmākāratayā punaḥ
vṛttivismaraṇaṁ samyak samādhirjñānasaṁjñakaḥ

nirvikāratayā *nirvikāra* mfn uniform, normal, unchangeable, unchanged,
nir- prefix, without
vikāra m. modification, agitation, alteration or deviation from any natural state, *-tayā* ness, through unchangeableness

vṛttyā 3/s/f *vṛtti* through activity, through function, conduct, working, being, mode of being, through disturbances in consciousness such as thoughts, perceptions, ripples, waves,

brahmākāratayā *brahmākāra* the state of being brahman alone,
tayā -ness

punaḥ again

vṛttivismaraṇam n. oblivion, forgetting, act of forgetting,

samyak mfn correct, accurate, proper, ind. properly, correctly, completely,

samādhirjñānasaṁjñakaḥ
samādhi m. profound or abstract meditation,
jñāna n. knowledge, higher knowledge, awareness,
saṁjñakaḥ mfn classified as, named, called, name of anything thought of as standing by itself,

124. A mode of being without any deviation or change of natural state, changeless; the state of being Brahman alone, senses withdrawn, mind still, everything forgotten including meditation. This is called *Samādhi* or *Jñānam.*

Comment: Meditating on the *svarūpa* (own nature) of *Brahman* is *Brahmākāra vritti.* Focused only on *Brahman* and nothing else is *nirvikāravritti.* When the meditation reaches the finality of even forgetting that the *sādhaka* (aspirant) is meditating on *Brahman*, that state is *samādhi* and that is called *jñāna.* I believe this is the final experience of non-duality, devoid of all objectivity and any sense of duality. [Internet comment by K. Ramakrishna]

इमञ्चाकृत्रिमानन्दं तावत् साधु समभ्यसेत् ।

वश्यो यावत् क्षणात् पुंसः प्रयुक्तः सन् भवेत् स्वयम् ।।१२५।।

imañcākṛtrimānandaṁ tāvat sādhu samabhyaset

vaśyo yāvat kṣaṇāt puṁsaḥ prayuktaḥ san bhavet svayam

imañcākṛtrimānandaṁ *imam* pron. 2/s/m this, *ca* and

akṛtrim- mfn natural, in-artificial,

-ānandam 2/s/m bliss, natural bliss

tāvat	ind. corel. as long
sādhu	mfn good, saint, noble, virtuous, pure, kind, excellent, obedient,
samabhyaset	1/s/opt/act he should exercise, practice *(sam-abhi-√as)*
vaśyaḥ	mfn humbled, submissive, dutiful, obedient, being under control,
yāvat	ind. corel. until
kṣaṇāt	5/s/m from a second, moment, twinkling of an eye, instant, momentarily, moment by moment,
puṁsaḥ	1/s/m 5/6/s/m *puṁs* of a person, of a man,
prayuktaḥ san	being undertaken, performed, begun, done,
bhavet	he/it should be or become 1/s/opt/act √*bhū*
svayam	own self,

125. And this natural bliss (of meditation) should be practised obediently and thoroughly until it can be performed to realize one's own Self moment by moment.

ततः साधननिर्मुक्तः सिद्धो भवति योगिराट् ।
तत्स्वरूपं न चैतस्य विषयो मनसो गिराम् ।।१२६।।

tataḥ sādhananirmuktaḥ siddho bhavati yogirāṭ
tatsvarūpaṁ na caitasya viṣayo manaso girām

tataḥ adv. from that time, then, due to that,
sādhananirmuktaḥ *sādhana-* n. instrument, means, realisation,
-nirmuktaḥ mfn set free, freed, liberated, free from every attachment, free from the means for realisation,
siddhaḥ mfn perfected, become perfect, successful, powerful,
bhavati 1/s/pres/act √*bhū* he becomes
yogirāṭ *yogi* + *ra* (comparative) best, 5/s/m from the best *yogi*
tat that
svarūpam own form, own nature, true nature
na not
ca and
etasya pron. 6/s/m or n of this
viṣayaḥ 1/s/m topic, subject, matter, case, theme,
manasaḥ 5/6/s/m *manas* of /from the mind
girām 2/s/f? speech, voice

126. Then he becomes perfected, best among yogis, free from practising the means for realisation, his own nature beyond mind or speech.

समाधौ क्रियमाणे तु विघ्नान्यायान्ति वै बलात् ।
अनुसन्धानराहित्यमालस्यं भोगलालसम् ।।१२७।।

samādhau kriyamāṇe tu vighnānyāyānti vai balāt
anusandhānarāhityamālasyaṁ bhogalālasam

लयस्तमश्चविक्षेपो रसास्वादश्च शून्यता ।
एवं यद्विघ्नबाहुल्यं त्याज्यं ब्रह्मविदा शनैः ।।१२८।।

layastamaścavikṣepo rasāsvādaśca śūnyatā
evaṁ yadvighnabāhulyaṁ tyājyaṁ brahmavidā śanaiḥ

samādhau	7/s/m in *samādhi,* during *samādhi,*
kriyamāṇe	7/s/m pres.part. being done, in being practised,
tu	ind. but, and,
vighnānyāyānti	*vighna* m. obstacle, hindrance, interruption
-anya	mfn different, other,
-āyānti	*1/pl/pres/ ā√yā* they arrive, approach, reach, enter,
vai	ind. indeed
balāt	5/s/m from force, power, strength,
anusandhānarāhityamālasyaṁ	*anusandhāna* n. plan, searching, investigation, inquiry,
rāhityam	1/s/n. being destitute of or free from or without,
ālasyam	2/s mfn idle, n. idleness
bhogalālasam	*bhoga* m. indulgence, enjoyment, sensual pleasure,
lālasam	2/s/ mfn delighting or absorbed in, eagerly longing for,
layastamaścavikṣepaḥ	

layas	m. repose, lying down, rest, indifference, mental inactivity,
-tamas	n. mental darkness, ignorance, gloom, illusion, dullness,
-ca	and
-vikṣepaḥ	1/s/m scattering, dispersion, agitation,
rasāsvādaśca	*rasāsvādaḥ* 1/s/m appreciation, sipping of juice, perception of pleasure,
-ca	and
śūnyatā	1/s/f emptiness, distraction, illusory nature, nothingness,
evam	ind. thus
yadvighnabāhulyam	*yat* which
-vighna	m. obstacle, hindrance, interruption
-bāhulyam	1/2/s/n abundance, variety, multitude, plenty, multiplicity, usual course or common order of things,
tyājyam	mfn to be sacrificed or given up or abandoned or quitted,
brahmavidā	3/s/m *brahmavid* mfn by metaphysical, vedic philosopher, knowing the one *Brahman,*
śanaiḥ	3/pl/ *śana* calm, quiet, soft, softly, quietly, calmly, gently,

127, 128. In practising *samādhi* difficulties inevitably enter. These are described as absence of inquiry, laziness, wishing for sensual pleasure, sleep, dullness, agitation, perception of pleasure and experience of nothingness. These common obstacles should be gently given up by one seeking to know Brahman.

भाववृत्त्या हि भावत्वं शून्यवृत्त्या हि शून्यता ।
ब्रह्मवृत्त्या हि पूर्णत्वं तथा पूर्णत्वमभ्यसेत् ॥१२९॥

bhāvavṛttyā hi bhāvatvaṁ śūnyavṛttyā hi śūnyatā
brahmavṛttyā hi pūrṇatvaṁ tathā pūrṇatvamabhyaset

bhāvavṛttyā *bhāva-* m. true condition or state, conduct, thing, state, object
-vṛttyā 3/s/f mode of life or conduct, activity, mental activity, movements of the mind, thinking of an object,
hi because, therefore, so, certainly, indeed, since,
bhāva+tva+m 2/s/m object, + having the nature of, 'objectness'
śūnyavṛttyā *śūnya-* mfn vacant, blank, empty, void,
vṛttyā as above, thinking of a void or nothing,
hi as above
śūnyatā f. nothingness, emptiness, absence of mind,
brahmavṛttyā *brahma-* Supreme Spirit, Absolute, one self-existent Spirit
vṛttyā as above,
hi as above
pūrṇa+ tva + m mfn complete, full, thorough, filled with, full of, perfect,
tathā ind. so, such, thus
pūrṇatvamabhyaset *pūrṇa+ tva + m* perfect + having the nature of, perfection, 2/s/mfn
abhyaset *abhi +* √*as* to concentrate one's attention upon, practise, study, 1/s/opt/act he should practise, study, give his attention to,

129. When one thinks of an object then mental activity to do with the nature of that object arises. When thinking of nothing then the mind is empty. When the mind is on Brahman then there is perfection. Therefore constantly practise being aware of Brahman in order to attain perfection.

ये हि वृत्तिं जहत्येनां ब्रह्माख्यां पावनीं पराम् ।

वृथैव ते तु जीवन्ति पशुभिश्च समा नराः ।।१३०।।

ye hi vṛttiṁ jahatyenāṁ brahmākhyāṁ pāvanīṁ parām

vṛthaiva te tu jīvanti paśubhiśca samā narāḥ

ye	1/pl/m who
hi	because, therefore, so, certainly, indeed, since,
vṛttim	2/s/f 3/s/f mode of life or conduct, activity, mental activity, movements of the mind,
jahati	1/s/pres √hā he renounces, neglects, disregards,
enām	enclitic pron. this
brahmākhyām	2/s/f named Brahman
pāvanīm	2/s which eradicates (purifying)
parām	2/s supreme, or ind. supremely,
vṛthā	ind. in vain, futile, *eva* indeed,
te	pron. 1/pl/m they
tu	but,
jīvanti	1/pl/pres/act √*jī* they live,
paśubhiḥ	3/pl/ by, with, animals, beasts,
ca	and
samāḥ	1/pl/ the same, equal, even,
narāḥ	1/pl/m persons, people,

130. But those who disregard this supreme purifying Brahman live in vain and on the same level as animals.

⧈

ये हि वृत्तिं विजानन्ति ज्ञात्वापि वर्धयन्ति ये ।

ते वै सत्पुरुषा धन्या वन्द्यास्ते भुवनत्रये ॥१३१॥

ye hi vṛttiṁ vijānanti jñātvāpi vardhayanti ye

te vai satpuruṣā dhanyā vandyāste bhuvanatraye

ye	who
hi	for, since, indeed, therefore
vṛttiṁ	existing, state, way of behaving, being, mode of being, fluctuations of reflected consciousness, the waves of mental activities, mental modifications,
vijānanti	1/pl they learn or understand that, they become wise or learned,
jñātvā	having learnt or understood,
-api	also, even,
vardhayanti	1/pl they cause to increase or grow, magnify, expand,
ye	who
te	pron. those *vai* indeed, particle of emphasis or affirmation,
satpuruṣā	a good or virtuous man,
dhanyā	blessed, glorious, fortunate, auspicious,
vandyās	adorable, venerable, to be respected or regarded or saluted,
te	they
bhuvanatraye	7/s in the three worlds, (heaven, atmosphere and earth,)

131. Blessed indeed are those adorable ones who understanding the fluctuation of reflected consciousness become wise and continue to grow in this way. They are to be respected everywhere.

येषां वृत्तिः समा वृद्धा परिपक्वा च सा पुनः ।

ते वै सद्ब्रह्मतां प्राप्ता नेतरे शब्दवादिनः ॥१३२॥

yeṣāṁ vṛttiḥ samā vṛddhā paripakvā ca sā punaḥ

te vai sadbrahmatāṁ prāptā netare śabdavādinaḥ

yeṣām pron. 6/pl whose

vṛttiḥ 1/s mode of life or conduct, being, activities, mental activities, state, condition, general usage, constant, unchanged,

samā mfn equal, same, even, match, equivalent,

vṛddhā mfn distinguished by, increased, developed, large, increased,

paripakvā mfn professional, fully digested, quite ripe, accomplished, mature, completely burnt, perfect,

ca and

sā that

punaḥ again

te they

vai indeed

sadbrahmatām fem abstract noun, ever existent brahman-ness

prāptā mfn 1/s/f valid, met with, complete, proper, accomplished,

na not

itare 7/s/ *itara* in other, different from, another,

śabdavādinaḥ 5/s from talking about words,

132. Those whose state of being has become even, developed and mature realise the ever-existent Brahman, not those who merely play with words.

⧈

कुशला ब्रह्मवार्तायां वृत्तिहीनाः सुरागिणः ।

तेऽप्यज्ञानतया नूनं पुनरायान्ति यान्ति च ।।१३३।।

kuśalā brahmavārtāyāṁ vṛttihīnāḥ surāgiṇaḥ

te'pyajñānatayā nūnaṁ punarāyānti yānti ca

kuśalā *kuśala* mfn 1/s/f skilful, competent, able, clever, adroit,

brahmavārtāyām *brahma* Brahman

-vārtāyām 7/s/f *vārtā* topic, conversing, in talking about Brahman

vṛttihīnāḥ *vṛtti* mode of life or conduct, being, activities, mental activities, state, condition, constant, unchanged, movements of the mind,

-hīnāḥ 1/pl/m mfn insufficient, inferior to, defective, poor, destitute of, without activities, free from movements of the mind,

surāginaḥ *rāginaḥ* 1/s attached, *su-* well, greatly

te'pyajñānatayā *te* pron. they

-api also,

-ajñāna- ignorance

-tayā suffix of so many kinds

nūnam ind. indeed, just, at present, at once, therefore, assuredly,

punaḥ again

āyānti 1/pl/pres *yā* to go + prefix *ā* they come,

yānti 1/pl/pres *yā* to go they go

ca and

133. Those who are clever in talking about Brahman but deficient in conduct (including mental activities), who are greatly attached, or are in ignorance of so many possible kinds, assuredly come and go again and again.

◻

निमेषार्धं न तिष्ठन्ति वृत्तिं ब्रह्ममयीं विना ।

यथा तिष्ठन्ति ब्रह्माद्याः सनकाद्याः शुकादयः ।।१३४।।

nimeṣārdhaṁ na tiṣṭhanti vṛttiṁ brahmamayīṁ vinā

yathā tiṣṭhanti brahmādyāḥ sanakādyāḥ śukādayaḥ

nimeṣārdham	2/s in half a twinkling of the eyes, in an instant,
na	not,
tiṣṭhanti	1/s/pl √*sthā* they stand, stay, remain,
vṛttim	2/s *vṛtti* mode of life or conduct, being, activities, mental activities, state, existing, movements of the mind,
brahmamayīm	mfn consisting of *Brahman*
vinā	f. a lute, ind. except, without,
yathā	ind. as, like, because,
tiṣṭhanti	1/s/pl √*sthā* they stand, stay, remain,
brahmā	*Brahmā*
	1/pl beginning with
sanaka	*Sanaka*
ādyāḥ	1/pl beginning with
śukāt	5/s from *Śuka*
ayaḥ	1/s thus, in this manner,

134. (The aspirant should) not be without the mind on Brahman, even for a moment. They should be steady like the sages beginning with Brahmā, Sanaka, Śuka and others.

कार्ये कारणतायाता कारणे नहि कार्यता ।

कारणत्वं ततो गच्छेत् कार्याभवे विचारतः ॥१३५॥

kārye kāraṇatāyātā kāraṇe nahi kāryatā

kāraṇatvaṁ tato gacchet kāryābhave vicārataḥ

kārye	7/s n. in the act, deed, function, effect, result,
kāraṇatāyātā	*kāraṇatā* 1/s/f the causality, causation, the nature of the cause
-āyātā	1/s/f mfn stretched, lengthened, extending, extended, spread over, directed towards,
kāraṇe	7/s in the cause, instrumentality, motive, cause of anything,
na	not
hi	ind. because, for, surely, indeed, since,
kāryatā	1/s/f being an effect, relation or state of an effect,
kāraṇatvam	2/s having the nature of a cause, causality,
tataḥ	ind. due to that, therefore, from that, from that time,
gacchet	1/s/pres/act/opt it should go (disappear), die,
kāryābhave	*kārya* n. act, deed, function, effect
-abhave	7/s/m in the absence, in the non-existence, in the negation, in the absence of the effect,
vicārataḥ	mfn considered, deliberated, reasoned, reflected,

135. The nature of the cause extends into the effect but the nature of the effect does not extend into the cause. Therefore, reasonably, in the absence of an effect the cause disappears.

◻

अथ शुद्धं भवेद्वस्तु यद्वै वाचामगोचरम् ।
द्रष्ठव्यं मृद्घटेनैव दृष्टान्तेन पुनः पुनः ॥१३६॥

atha śuddhaṁ bhavedvastu yadvai vācāmagocaram
draṣṭhavyaṁ mṛdghaṭenaiva dṛṣṭāntena punaḥ punaḥ

atha	ind. now, so, hence,
śuddham	2/s mfn pure (unmodified), free from, faultless, unmixed,
bhavedvastu	*bhavet* he/it should become 1/s/opt/act *bhū*
-vastu	n. item, object, thing, any really existing or abiding substance or essence, real, matter, right thing, worthy object, natural disposition,
yat	which *vai* indeed
vācām	6/pl/m *vāc* of words,
agocaram	2/s mfn or n. beyond the cognizance of the senses, the not being seen, mfn unattainable, beyond the range,
draṣṭhavyam	2/s fut. part. to be seen or examined or investigated,
mṛdghaṭenaiva	*mṛd* f. earth, soil, clay, loam,
-ghaṭena	3/s *ghaṭa* m. a jar, pitcher, jug, as an earthenware pitcher is just earth in a different form,
eva	indeed, only, alone,
dṛṣṭāntena	3/s/m by the standard, type, example, instance, allegory, paragon, end or aim of what is seen, by the example
punaḥ punaḥ	again and again,

136. Now purified, he should 'be' that reality beyond the realm of words. This is to be seen again and again in the same way as the real substance of a pot is seen to be earth.

अनेनैव प्रकारेण वृत्तिर्ब्रह्मात्मिका भवेत् ।

उदेति शुद्धचित्तानां वृत्तिज्ञानं ततः परम् ॥१३७॥

anenaiva prakāreṇa vṛttirbrahmātmikā bhavet
udeti śuddhacittānāṁ vṛttijñānaṁ tataḥ param

anenaiva *anena* 3/s by this
-eva ind. indeed, alone, only,
prakāreṇa 3/s n. treatment, discussion, explanation, a subject, topic, question, (a) typical performance, thinking like this,
vṛttirbrahmātmikā *vṛttiḥ* 2/s *vṛtti* - mode of life or conduct, being, activities, mental activities, state, condition, general usage,
-brahma Brahman
-ātmikā 1/s/f. based on, characterized by, pertaining to the Self, having the nature of *Brahman,* state of being *Brahman*
bhavet he should become
udeti he arises, arises from, proceeds, comes up, comes out of
śuddha-cittānāṁ 6/pl of those whose minds are pure,
vṛtti-jñānaṁ awareness of being, knowledge of being,
tataḥ param phrase - thereupon, after that, beyond that,

137. For those whose minds are pure, through this method alone one becomes as Brahman. Then the state of awareness as Brahman arises.

कारणं व्यतिरेकेण पुमानादौ विलोकयेत्
अन्वयेन पुनस्तद्धि कार्ये नित्यं प्रपश्यति ॥१३८॥

kāraṇaṁ vyatirekeṇa pumānādau vilokayet
anvayena punastaddhi kārye nityaṁ prapaśyati

kāraṇam	2/s/n cause, reason, means, motive,
vyatirekeṇa	3/s/m by the *vyatireka* method of negation, distinction, separation, exclusion, contrast to,
pumān	m a man, a person,
ādau	7/s/m *ādi,* in the beginning, at the start,
vilokayet	1/s/opt/act/*vilok* he should examine, consider, observe, have regard to, study, look at,
anvayena	3/s/m *anvaya* by logical connection of cause and effect, relation,
punaḥ	adv. again
tat	pron. that
hi	ind. for, surely, indeed, because, since,
kārye	7/s/n. in deed, function, act, mfn what has to be done, fit to be done, to be imposed or offered or bought, an effect, result, motive, object, aim, purpose, in the effect,
nityam	adv. always, eternally, ever, or mfn 2/s eternal, perpetual,
prapaśyati	1/s/pres/act *pra* √*paś* he foresees, judges, understands, discerns, perceives, takes for, knows,

138. A person should firstly, consider the cause through *vyatireka* (a method of negation) and again through *anvaya* (logical connection of cause and effect) because in the effect he knows the eternal cause.

◻

कार्ये हि कारणं पश्येत् पश्चात् कार्यं विसर्जयेत् ।

कारणत्वं ततो गच्छेदवशिष्टं भवेन्मुनिः ॥१३९॥

kārye hi kāraṇaṁ paśyet pāścāt kāryaṁ visarjayet
kāraṇatvaṁ tato gacchedavaśiṣṭaṁ bhavenmuniḥ

kārye 7/s/n. *kārya* in deed, function, act, mfn what has to be done, fit to be done, to be imposed or offered or bought, an effect, result, motive, object, aim, purpose, in the effect,

hi ind. for, surely, indeed, because, since,

kāraṇam 2/s/n cause, reason, means, motive,

paśyet 1/s/opt/act √*paś* he should see

pāścāt ind. after, afterwards, backwards, later, subsequently,

kāryam 2/s/n the effect, the result,

visarjayet 1/s/opt/caus/act *vi*√*sṛj* he should discharge, emit, set free, release, let go, dismiss, despatch, abandon, relinquish, give up,

kāraṇatvam *2/s/* cause, reason, means, motive, + *tva* having the nature of,

tataḥ adv. resulting from that, due to that, therefore, from that, from that time, then,

gacchedavaśiṣṭaṁ *gacchet* 1/s/opt/act √*gam* he should go, it goes,

-avaśiṣṭam 2/s/mfn remaining, n. remainder, rest,

bhavet 1/s/opt/act √*bhū* he should be

muniḥ 1/s/m the sage

139. The cause may be seen in the effect. The result should be let go and since it has the nature of the cause or motive then that too will be released. The sage is thus whatever remains.

⧈

भावितं तीव्रवेगेन यद्वस्तु निश्चयात्मना ।

पुमांस्तद्धि भवेच्छीघ्रं ज्ञेयं भ्रमरकीटवत् ॥१४०॥

bhāvitaṁ tīvravegena yadvastu niścayātmanā
pumāṁstaddhi bhavecchīghraṁ jñeyaṁ bhramarakīṭavat

bhāvitam mfn 2/s soaked in, devoted to, exhibited, made to become, directed towards, transformed into, infused, caused to be,
tīvravegena *tīvra* mfn intensive, acute, keen, fierce, severe, hot, excessive,
vegena 3/s *vega* by impulse, speed, velocity, agitation, force, momentum,
yat pron. which, what,
vastu 1/s/n thing, item, object,
niścayāt 5/s from or through certainty, conviction, decision,
manā 3/s/n by/with *mana* thought, view, belief,
pumān 1/s/m a man *tat* pron. that
hi ind. because, for, since,
bhavet he should be, become,
śīghram adv. quickly,
jñeyam 2/s mfn to be known or understood or learnt or perceived,
bhramara- m. bee, bumble-bee, wasp,
kīṭa m. worm, caterpillar, insect,
-vat suffix - as, like, like the wasp and the worm❊
❊refers to a belief in which an insect dragged into a wasp-hole, constantly thinking of the wasp because of fear, becomes a wasp.

140. Whatever a man is devoted to with intense force through sincere conviction, that he quickly becomes. This should be understood through the story of the wasp and the worm.

◘

अदृश्यं भावरूपञ्च सर्वमेव चिदात्मकम् ।

सावधानतया नित्यं स्वात्मानं भावयेद्बुधः ॥१४१

adṛśyaṁ bhāvarūpañca sarvameva cidātmakam

sāvadhānatayā nityaṁ svātmānaṁ bhāvayedbudhaḥ

adṛśyam	*2/s* the not seen, the invisible,
bhāvarūpam	*2/s* mfn the form or appearance of transient reality
ca	and
sarvam	all, everything,
eva	indeed, only, alone,
cidātmakam	*2/s* consisting of pure thought, of the nature of consciousness,
sāvadhāna	mfn with an attentive mind, carefully,
-tayā	by that, with that, of so many kinds or divisions,
nityam	2/s mfn eternal, constant, perpetual, ever, always,
svātmānam	own Self
bhāvayet	1/s/opt /caus/ should cause to be or become, call into existence or life, produce, create, animate, enliven, devote one's self to, practise, present to the mind, think about,
budhaḥ	1/s/m awaking, intelligent, clever, wise, a sage,

141. A wise man should constantly think of the visible, the invisible and everything else as his own Self, pure consciousness.

दृश्यं ह्यदृश्यतां नीत्वा ब्रह्माकारेणा चिन्तयेत ।
विद्वान्नित्यसुखे तिष्टेद्धिया चिद्रसपूर्णया ॥१४२॥

dṛśyaṁ hyadṛśyatāṁ nītvā brahmkāreṇā cintayet
vidvānnityasukhe tiṣṭeddhiyā cidrasapūrṇayā

dṛśyam 2/s mfn, n. the seen, the visible, the splendid
hi for (as) , since, because, emphasis, filler,
adṛśyatām 2/s/f the unseen, invisible,
nītvā gerund, having passed, bringing, leading (the soul), having caused a condition in someone,
brahmākāreṇā *brahman*
-ākāreṇā 3/s/m by, with, *ākāra* external aspect of the body, figure, shape, appearance, Brahman with physical aspects,
cintayet 1/s/opt/act √*bhū* should consider as, think of
vidvānnityadukhe *vidvān* 'one who knows', the wise one, the illumined soul, the wise
-nitya ever
sukhe 7/s in happiness
tiṣṭet 1/s/opt/act √*sthā* he should stay, remain, abide, exist
dhiyā ind. mentally, by thought, by intelligence
cidrasapūrṇayā *cid* (of) consciousness
rasa (of) essence
pūrṇayā 3/s *pūrna* mfn complete, full, filled with, abundant, perfect

142. A wise man should think of the visible as a physical indication or aspect of the invisible Brahman. The mind should ever abide in happiness with the fullness of the essence of consciousness.

◻

एभिरङ्गैः समायुक्तो राजयोग उदाहृतः ।
किञ्चित्पक्वकषायाणां हठयोगेन संयुतः ।।१४३।।

ebhiraṅgaiḥ samāyukto rājayoga udāhṛtaḥ
kiñcitpakvakaṣāyāṇāṁ haṭhayogena saṁyuktaḥ

ebhiḥ 3/pl pron. by/with these

aṅgaiḥ 3/pl *aṅga* by/with limbs, parts, steps,

samāyuktaḥ 1/s/ mfn committed, ready, prepared, joined, devoted to,

rājayoga the Royal Way known as *Rājayoga*

udāhṛtaḥ 1/s mfn declared, said, named, called, described

kiñcitpakvakaṣāyāṇām *kiñcit* anyone

pakva mfn cooked, burnt, mature, ripe for decay,

kaṣāyāṇām 6/pl mfn whose, attachment to worldly objects, stain or impurity or sin cleaving to the soul,

haṭhayogena 3/s by/with *haṭhayoga* yoga of (physical) force,

saṁyuktaḥ 1/s/mfn joined together, combined,

143. The steps of the system called *Rājayoga* have been described. Those whose attachment to worldly objects is ripened and ready to fall may combine them with *Hathayoga*.

Note: The *hathayoga* referred to is likely that of Patanjali who originated the 15 principles that have been described. The wikipedia entry on it contains the following quote. Note that no extremes of any kind are mentioned.

'Patanjali begins discussion of Asanas (आसन, posture) by defining it in verse 46 of Book 2, as follows, स्थिरसुखमासनम् ॥४६॥ Translation 1: An asana is what is steady and pleasant.

Translation 2: Motionless and Agreeable form (of staying) is Asana (yoga posture).
— Yoga Sutras II.46
Asana is thus a posture that one can hold for a period of time, staying relaxed, steady, comfortable and motionless. Patanjali does not list any specific asana, except the terse

suggestion, "posture one can hold with comfort and motionlessness". Āraṇya translates verse II.47 of Yoga sutra as, "asanas are perfected over time by relaxation of effort with meditation on the infinite"; this combination and practice stops the quivering of body. The posture that causes pain or restlessness is not a yogic posture. Other secondary texts studying Patanjali's sutra state that one requirement of correct posture is to keep breast, neck and head erect (proper spinal posture).

परिपक्वं मनो येषां केवलोऽयं च सिद्धिदः ।

गुरुदैवतभक्तानां सर्वेषां सुलभो जवात् ॥१४४।

paripakvaṁ mano yeṣāṁ kevalo'yaṁ ca siddhidaḥ
gurudaivatabhaktānāṁ sarveṣāṁ sulabho javāt

paripakvam 2/s completely burnt, completely cooked, mature, fully ripe,

manaḥ 1/s the mind,

yeṣāṁ 6/pl/m pron. of whom

kevalah 1/s mfn alone, only, entire, unmingled, entirely, whole,

yam 2/s pron. which, who,

ca and,

siddhidaḥ conferring felicity or beatitude, or perfection

gurudaivatabhaktānāṁ *guru* (to) teacher

-daivata relating to the gods, (of) divine,

-bhaktānāṁ *bhakta* 6/pl mfn of the devoted, worshipping,

sarveṣāṁ 6/pl/pron. of all

sulabhaḥ 1/s/ mfn answering to, easy, useful, easy to obtain, feasible,

javāt 5/s/m java from swiftness, velocity, speed, impulse,
mfn swift, speedily,

144. For he whose mind is completely burnt (purified), this (Rājayoga) alone confers perfection. This is easily and swiftly attained by those having devotion to their guru and the divine.

□

Bibliography

A Sanskrit-English Dictionary – Sir Monier Monier-Williams, Motilal Banarsidass, Delhi, 1993

(Apte) The Student's Sanskrit English Dictionary – VS Apte, Motilal Banarsidass, Delhi 1997

Atmabodha Swami Chinmayananda - Central Chinmaya Mission Trust Mumbai

(B) Sanskrit Manual – Roderick S. Bucknell –Motilal Banarsidass, Delhi 1996

(C) Ashtavakra Gita translated by Hari Prasad Shastri –Shanti Sadan London 1961

(F) Teach yourself Sanskrit –Michael Coulson, Teach Yourself Books, Hodder, England 2001

The Sanskrit Language – an Introductory Grammar and Reader, WH Maurer, Curzon, 1995

(G) A Concise Dictionary of Indian Philosophy – John Grimes, SUNY, NY, 1996

(H) A practical aid for the study of Sanskrit Dhātus – The School of Economic Science, London 2003

(HH)Quotations from his Holiness śrī śāntānanda saraswatī, śankarācārya

(I) Dhātu Pātha – Hill and Harrison – Duckworth 1991

(J) The roots, verb-forms and primary derivatives of the Sanskrit language –WD Whitney reprint 1994 Motilal Banarsidass Delhi

(K) Wikipedia

(LM) Quotations from Mr. Leon McLaren in various publications

Laghu Kaumudi of Varadaraja James R Ballantyne reprint 1995 Motilal Banarsidass, Delhi

The Siddhanta Kaumudi of Bhattoji Dikshita (Vasu) reprint 1982 Motilal Banarsidass, Delhi

(O) A Sanskrit Manual (for High Schools) Parts 1 and 2, R.Antoine S.J. Xavier Pubn. Calcutta,

(P) Pāṇini

(Q) Materials for a Dictionary of the Prajñāpāramitā Literature, Edward Conze, Suzuki Research Foundation 1973

(R) A Sanskrit-English Dictionary AA Macdonell, 1924 MLBD

A Sanskrit Grammar for Students A.A. Macdonell reprint 1997 Motilal Banarsidass, Delhi

(S) śaṅkara

(T) Svetasvatara Upanishad Trans. Swami Tyagisananda, Sri Ramakrishna Math Chennai 2006,

(U) The Philosophy of the Panchadasi Swami Krishnananda, The Divine Life Society, Rishikesh

(V) Bhaktivedanta Vedabase

(W) Encyclopaedia of the Hindu World, Gaṅga Rām Garg, Concept Publishing, New Delhi, 1992

(X) Teach Yourself Sanskrit, Michael Coulson, Hodder and Stoughton Educational, London 2004

A Concise Elementary Grammar of the Sanskrit Language, Jan Gonda, The Univ. Alabama Press 1966

A Sanskrit Grammar for Students A.A. Macdonell reprint 1997 Motilal Banarsidass, Delhi

Devavāṇīpraveśikā – An introduction to the Sanskrit Language – RP Goldman & SJS Goldman 1980 et al, University of California, Berkeley

Introduction to Sanskrit, parts 1 and 2 - Thomas Egenes 1989, 1985 Motilal Banarsidass, Delhi

Pāṇini –His Description of Sanskrit Jag Deva Singh

Sanskrit Grammar for Beginners – Second Edition – Max Müller –Hippocrene Books, New York 2004 (M)

Sanskrit Grammar – William Dwight Whitney – Bodhi Leaves Corp. Delhi reprint 1990 (W)

School of Economic Science London Sanskrit Faculty -numerous texts

Self Knowledge - Swāmi Nikhilānanda Sri Ramakrishna Math, Madras

The Penguin Dictionary of English Grammar – R.L. Trask , Penguin 2000 (X)

The Bhagavad Gita - Winthrop Sergeant SUNY 1994

Bhagavad Gita translated by Swami Gambhirananda,

Advaita Ashrama fifth impression May 2000

Secondary Suffixes in Sanskrit Grammar Dr. D K Das Sanskrit Book Depot 2002

A Sanskrit Grammar for Students Arthur A Macdonell Motilal Banarsidass, Delhi

A Sanskrit Reader Charles Rockwell Lanman 1885 Motilal Banarsidass, Delhi

I would like to gratefully acknowledge the generous and thorough help of Helen Miller and Paul Phillips for proofing the work, suggestions and other improvements.

www.ingramcontent.com/pod-product-compliance
Lightning Source LLC
Chambersburg PA
CBHW080412230426
43662CB00016B/2384
9780994104496